The California Dream (1971)

—Based on a True Story—

Written By:
Jacob Sparks

Illustrated By:
Gennaro Pollice

Dedicated to Bob —

I'd walk to California to see you again.

Contents

Introduction

My first encounter with Mike was unforgettable. It was at the junior high school, Monday morning, with teachers and students busily traversing the halls. Mike had been publicly insulted by a rogue and rude fellow student on the Friday before in front of a crowd of his peers. Having fumed, reliving the disgrace over the entire weekend, Mike was now steadfastly resolved to redeem his honor in a brash act, every bit as public as was his humiliation. He marched directly up to his enemy in the middle of the main hall and punched him in the face with all the strength he had! Game on! The boy who got hit —actually the whole school — was in shock; everyone except Mike, who hadn't slept well since Friday. The overwhelming boredom of another day at school vanished, as the fists flew. Adrenaline flowed through the halls like the Colorado River! We were liberated, thanks to Mike who earned celebrity status for at least a couple weeks. Later, after coming to know Mike, I was amazed at how out of character his attack on this boy had been. Mike was pathologically shy. If a teacher asked him a question in class, Mike's eyes would widen in a "fight or flight" anxiety and he would freeze, not even answering the teacher. I too was shy, though not to the degree Mike was, and hence we were very compatible.

After an initial acquainting of sitting together on a bus, again Mike deviated from his routine introversion and began to persistently show up at my home. I think he had reached a point of desperation in which he believed he had to either escape his shell or resign himself to the sad life of a loner. Still, by no means had his shyness been eradicated. He reached out to me, looking for his first friend, yet was still plagued by his tentative posture. He would come to my house and knock at the door. My mother would answer. He would wait at the door until I arrived and then just stand there in silence. We were both socially uncomfortable and quickly became each other's all-in-all, directing the love and comradery meant for many people to just one person. We became inseparable.

As a team, our confidence grew and we began the exodus from social reclusion. In the summer months we spent much of our time at Lewis' Lake, a popular swimming hole a few miles down the road. We became ardent fans of rock-and-roll, which was the obsession of the day ('60s and '70s). But our greatest retreat was without bounds—the derelict VW van in Mike's yard, underneath the big maple tree, which had been put out of its misery years earlier. Our imaginations had free reign as we devoted countless hours sitting in the pitiful rusted relic, planning her resurrection and how she would transport us in appropriate hippie fashion to our Shangri-La (California). The prospect of settling down somewhere and taking on a steady job, of course, had no appeal. We would stop in select towns along the way for a few days, doing menial work, only long enough to provide food and gas money. Then, like coveted yet elusive rolling stones, move on. Forsaken girls with badly broken hearts would be the only sad aspect of this glorious pilgrimage. Surely they would heal… in time.

Our folks had undetectable levels of concern regarding our volatile plans as they considered them to have little chance of seeing the light of day. It's true, the van would never run again. The California dream was another matter.

Chapter I
Lewis' Lake

Mike and I had somehow survived the rigors of high school and were free. Really free! Maybe too free. All youth, I believe, yearn for freedom from the time of their first spanking, or maybe their first set of wheels, around age three. Some degree of parental rebellion is reliable. We want to cut the cord. But as the reality of life on our own drew closer, Mike and I shared a strong sense of insecurity, though we never admitted it. We would boldly toss around prospects and options we might pursue: an electrician apprenticeship, maybe the military. I believe this talk served to allay the growing concern we had in managing our lives on our own. The parental tether we had vowed so long to sever began to lose its sinister aura. We started to realize the tether actually had some benefits. Like food. TV. A bed. Our own room. And money. Wow, how could we have been *so* wrong for *so* many years? Our more privileged classmates would go right on to college and never miss a beat. Another four years of abundant tethers and security. They didn't have to hit the bricks like the working class kids of the sixties and seventies did!

Mike and I conceived a strategy to deal with the looming crisis. Make that pilgrimage to California! After all, we were *men* now… shaving, etc. I realized the notion made little sense but it provided a comfort that was altogether absent in the legitimate career arena. Besides, *everyone* was doing it. There must be something extremely cool out there, we reasoned. This would be our stay of execution! I guess you can see why we weren't slated for college.

Neither of us had a vehicle (operable), so hitchhiking would be the mode of transportation. Luckily, begging rides was not only popular during this era but actually an honorable means of commuting among hippies and "love children". But, really, two naïve Midwest boys hitchhiking clear across the country with no family along the way or at our destination? And just exactly where was our destination? And why? How long would we stay?

"Lewis'?" suggested Mike. "Sure," I replied. Seemed like a reasonable escape. Forget California and careers for now....

The lake was packed. It was the first part of June and the weather was perfect. More importantly, I scanned the beach and sure enough, there she was! Kim and I were, seriously, girlfriend and boyfriend. At least that was my perspective. Kim was a little more tepid in her view of our relationship. I had many previous love interests in my short stint in the field and typically the girl was stricken with me. Not so much with Kim. I knew what I had to do. There was a Tarzan rope suspended from a structure that was approximately 75 feet high. It was simply two six-inch round steel poles that rose up out of the water, several feet apart, joined with another six inch round cross arm at the top. There were only 2 guys who could accomplish the feat and I was one of them. Shinnying up one of the poles to the top cross arm, precariously navigating across to a midway point, then standing up with nothing to hold for balance, I would dive! Sounds fairly straight-forward, but not so. I speculate only a tiny fraction of the population could manage the seventy-five foot vertical climb to begin with. The life threatening dive itself was relatively easy. But — land wrong from this height and you could burst your lungs or break your back! Negotiating that cross arm was next to impossible. Crossing it was extremely difficult (as the pipe was round), and to achieve a standing position defied all laws of physics. Further compounding the production was the ever-present knowledge there was zero room for error.

From the moment the maniac (usually me) approached and latched onto one of the poles like a tree frog, two things spontaneously occurred. One, within seconds, the crowd took notice and utter silence prevailed. The beach instantly transformed into a Barnum & Bailey circus and I was the main attraction: a small, death-defying figure

Lewis' Lake

whose every movement was being captured by the wide-eyed audience.Secondly, the reality of this act gripped me and I knew I was walking the plank. The captain had his gun pointed at my head. There could be no retreat. Had I surrendered to fear and slithered back down the pole, I would be banished from Lewis' Lake. All hope to dwell amongst my beach peers would be forever lost as would be any prospect of Kim as my future wife. In retrospect, I've got to say the dive from the tower was one of the most insane things I've ever seen, much less done. I have no idea why the lake owner or lifeguards allowed something so dangerous. I had performed the feat on numerous occasions and each time, as I was traversing the scary crossbar, I promised myself, in a nervous whisper, I'd never do it again. The reward for success, however, was tremendous. The entire rest of the day, people would approach me with compliments or comments … "Aren't you the guy who dove from the tower?" "Yes", I would answer modestly, like Superman — on break.

Of course my passion and motive in risking death in front of a crowd was Kim. Sadly, she never seemed too impressed. I wondered if slipping and whacking the back of my head on the cross arm on the way down — hitting the water limp and unconscious — might do the trick. With the crowd frozen in hushed horror, would she run and cling to my body as they carried me away on the stretcher?

Chapter 2
Carrie and Cassie

Soon after the bond was established with Mike and me, our debut into society and the world seemed to flourish. It was as though this union was the missing link to our liberation. We quickly added a few others to our elite and exclusive group. Before I introduce them I want to ensure the reader has a clear picture of Mike, as this book begins and ends with him. Contrary to the violent attack on his junior high school adversary, Mike was quiet, tender and shy. The fight had been a stark deviation from his normal disposition and in all the ensuing decades I have known Mike, I never saw any additional act of violence or even mild aggression.

Mike was average height and weight, as was I. He had a distinctly casual look with a relaxed gait, long hair (touching the top of his shoulders), and substantial bangs which were swept to the side but hung low enough to partially obscure his vision (and also provide a hiding place from social encounters). His eyes were large with an innocent puppy-dog look and a third of one of his front teeth had been broken and was missing. Mike was not exactly a pretty-boy, male model type. He quickly became my best friend. His big eyes and shyness were wide open for abuse by me and our other new friends, an act we frequently indulged ourselves in. Mike, however, was not defenseless and would respond in kind with some notable practical jokes of his own. At the risk of sounding vain, I think girls were a little quicker to notice me, however Mike never seemed to have any difficulty procuring a date — and with girls who were exceptionally pretty. I think it was that lost, puppy-dog look.

The handful of friends we collected became near and dear. They too were not popular. We were all a good fit, a rag-tag group made for each other. I became the group leader, I think more by way of default than qualifications. Rick Chadwick ('Chad') was outgoing, vivacious, ornery, and totally devoted to me. He would do anything I asked. He was short and a little pudgy and had the most beautiful coal-black, naturally curly hair. I don't think he even combed it. He could have paid a hairstylist a $100 and not got something so perfect.

Ronnie Heilman was another dear comrade, fourteen years old at our initial acquainting as were the rest of us, give or take. Ronnie's dad was a rough and tough no-nonsense steel-worker, absolutely uncompromising and mean. Ronnie's mom, conversely, was the sweetest, most peaceful woman imaginable. She was a peach, ever-faithful to restore our cash reserves and treats. She taught at the business college in Davenport, Iowa, a city about 10 miles down the road from our smaller suburb. She over-mothered Ronnie, I believe, to compensate for his father's cruel actions and demeanor. Ronnie consequently grew up with conflicting manifestations of these two influences. He had a tendency to be overly sensitive and soft-hearted. At other times you could see him struggling to be tough, like his dad. It didn't matter. He too became a good buddy.

Ronnie, Mike and I routinely hung out together. I was the common link as Mike and Ronnie had an ongoing personality conflict. Nothing serious, they were simply opposites. Mike was a "regular Joe" while I think Ronnie aspired to do lofty things someday. I scored somewhere between the two on the MMPI test and thereby coupled our trio in a strong bond.

Ronnie was intelligent, unique, unpredictable, and fun to be around. Peculiar and eccentric, but fun. A non-conformist. You never knew what he might do. For example, one day Ronnie came by Mike's house. He disclosed to us a bounty of 10 dollars his mother had given him. He wanted to know if we cared to join him in an excursion to Davenport to spend the cash. The three of us hitchhiked into town in the dead of winter with roughly 6 inches of snow and slush on the roads. Again, hitchhiking was popular during this time, at least for many young people. Of course, Mike and I wanted to do normal, typical things with the $10 Ronnie had kindly given a community status. Things like getting hamburgers and fries, playing pinball, or going to a record shop to check out the Beatle's latest album. Ronnie, however, was not "normal". He insisted we go to a second hand store. Bummer! Mike and I were in misery. Of all the fun things we could be doing or eating and Ronnie had us in a smelly store full of used clothes, toasters and furniture! I knew what had spawned this. His identity crisis, mom versus dad. Ronnie was to deal with those readily-apparent, opposing inclinations his entire life. As far as I know, he never found a happy medium.

Mike and I were praying whatever Ronnie bought would leave enough money for something sane people could enjoy. Not so. Ronnie spent the entire $10 on a beat-up old relic of a wooden wheel chair! Another bummer! Mike and I were both disappointed but not surprised. Ronnie, I'm sure, was satisfying both his father's and mother's teachings. Doing something crazy, yet being thoughtful and thrifty in making his purchase at a second-hand store!

Youthful spirits soon overwhelmed our depression. Mike and I joined Ronnie in pushing each other down the middle of the street on the one-ways in downtown Davenport. People stared in disbelief. Hitching a ride back home was difficult with a big, clunky, wooden wheelchair in tow, but Ronnie adamantly refused to part with the thing. When we finally got home, Ronnie pushed the wheelchair up to the top of the huge, snow-covered hill by his house. The hill was nearly a sheer cliff on the south side ending in a roadside ditch — the side Ronnie was peering over. Ronnie frequently sought to exterminate his mother-sourced soft side in dangerous acts of "manhood". This was one of those times.

As Ronnie sat in the rickety wheel chair poised on the very edge of the hill, Mike yelled to him, "Don't do it, Ronnie!" Sounded just like his mom. He pushed off. The ride was indeed breathtaking. But not the way Ronnie had in mind. When the chair took its first hop and went airborne for about 20 feet I knew Ronnie was in serious trouble. He obviously hadn't thought the stunt through. He clung to the chair with a death grip, his face frozen in terror! I knew this exploit would end the day's activities, at least the ambulatory ones. The wheelchair's contact with the hill was limited, only touching down 4 or 5 times total, like a boulder tumbling down a steep mountain. I remember thinking it oddly appropriate Ronnie had chosen a wheelchair for this! When the chair finally came to a stop in the snow-filled ditch, Ronnie was lying 15 feet away, moaning. Mike and I ran to his side, laughing and reveling in the fact he had survived the mighty feat. That is, until we realized he had a significant injury, later revealed as a broken tailbone! Poor Ronnie, struggling to be tough….and he was just getting started…

At age 17, Ronnie left for San Francisco. He hitchhiked alone, still struggling with the two natures inside him. A couple of years earlier, around 15, he had bought a book by Sonny Barger, the famous (or infamous) founder of the Oakland, California Chapter of the Hell's Angels. He read and studied the book like a newfound religion, following the precepts and lifestyles of the angels strictly. One requirement of the Hell's Angels' dress code was blue jeans. But not any blue jeans. They had to be a new pair of Levis'. The angel must never wash them. The adherent must also pour a can of beer on them, urinate on the jeans, then drag the trousers around for several miles behind his motorcycle — clearly at odds with the personal hygiene standards we had learned in health class. Ronnie happily complied. Of course he didn't have a big Harley, but his little 75 cc dirt bike and the mud track behind his house sufficed. His poor mom would have died had she caught wind of this!

Ronnie was in San Francisco for several years searching for himself. Torn between John Lennon peace gatherings and the Hell's Angels! Scuba-diving in beautiful tropical waters or riding a 900 cc motorcycle 160 miles per hour down the interstate at 2:00 a.m.!

His mother called his bike "Kamikaze". In Ronnie's case that quasi – serious humor would prove somewhat prophetic. He would later lose an arm in a motorcycle crash. I loved Ronnie and also admired him but I don't think he knew either of those two things. I believe he would forever see himself as inadequate because of his father's berating. He looked up to me as a strong person. I was the pack leader. He revered me and I believe desperately sought my respect for him as a man, as he considered that prospect from his father to be unattainable. I maintained contact with Ronnie through our twenties then lost touch.

Recently, I was out west and found an address and phone number for Ronnie in Oregon's Willamette Valley. He would not return my calls. He wasn't aware I knew of his motorcycle accident and I feel that was the reason he avoided a reunion. Revealing his handicap to me would have been too much for him. I believe he thought it would have designated him a failure in my eyes.

Back to the summer of 1971. Mike and I were gearing up for another visit to Lewis' Lake. Blue jean "cut-offs" were the rule. Those and a few bucks were all we needed. No shirt, no shoes, no socks or sandals. We could run barefoot on gravel — at least we could by June. Aside from Lewis' Lake, rock concerts, food and girls, Mike and I longed to see the ocean. As Midwestern landlubbers we had a burning desire to swim in the Pacific. We had both concluded, however, the idea of hitchhiking over 2,000 miles to an uncertain destination with an unknown goal was too scary to pursue. We had to admit, Ronnie had outdone us, all by himself. Though the idea of going to California had powerful appeal, we gently placed the dream to rest in the VW van.

"You diving today?" Mike asked.

"I don't know," I replied. "I doubt it."

I didn't take that stunt as lightly as Mike (the spectator). Summer was well underway and the sun made Lewis' Lake as much a necessity as recreation. Kim was unusually absent from her spot on the beach. She babysat during the day for a family that lived adjacent to the lake and could usually be seen with 3 toddlers playing in the sand or coming or going with the little ones in tow. I always thought it was such a beautiful scene. It made her look so mature. We would usually lay on the blanket while watching the kids play. I thought maybe someday we'd be doing the same thing with our own children. Mike was usually there on the blanket with us — awkwardly. Mike, on the other hand, seemed quite comfortable and content, like a big Lab pup! But not today.

Kim's absence reduced the festivity level, at least initially.

"Mike, check it out," I said.

"Check what out?" He asked.

"Check what out!" I exclaimed. "Those two lovelies over there frolicking in the water!"

"Oh, yeah, yeah," Mike replied in an excited whisper, his eyes narrowing as he zeroed in on the prey. To our amazement and delight were two girls — incredibly beautiful girls — who looked about our age. Turns out they too had just graduated high school.

"Hey, where you going?" Mike yelled to me.

After briefly considering the mortality vs benefit ratio, I swam across the lake. The mere sight of these two girls gave me strength and I climbed the pole with exceptional agility and skill, balanced for a moment on the cross arm, checked out the girls, and dove. Yes they, like everyone else, had their eyes trained on me.

Soon afterwards I made it a point for me and Mike to wade close by where the girls were and heard the words I had paid dearly to hear, from quite possibly the prettiest girl to have ever graced the shores of Lewis' Lake.

Carrie and Cassie

"Aren't you the one who dove from up there?"

"Yeah", I said, very casually — as though that was my usual place to dive from (as contrasted with the diving board, far below, that the common people used)!

"Pretty cool," she said.

"Oh, thanks," I replied. "Are you new to the beach?" I asked, as though I didn't know.

"Yes," she said. "We're visiting from California. Our parents have friends that live here in the park. I'm Carrie and this is my sister, Cassie".

Oh my gosh, I thought! Mike and I have struck gold! Not only they're beautiful, they're from California! The Beach Boys were right — California girls *were* better! Fraternal twins, Carrie and Cassie were both stunning. I thought Carrie to be a little prettier and focused on her. I introduced myself and Mike to the girls and it was love at first sight — for all four of us. Carrie and I, Mike and Cassie. It prevails but certainly without logic. Selecting a girlfriend based entirely on physical attributes. Regardless, Mike and I followed our indiscriminate instincts and suddenly the beach had new appeal. We met daily with our new "girlfriends" and the relationships exploded with excitement and young love!

Chapter 3
The Long (distance) Goodbye

It was late July 1971. We had experienced the proverbial "summer love" and that inevitable time had come to say goodbye. Only 4 weeks with the twins had seemed like an eternity. Heaven on earth (and water)! We had spent all our days together on the beach and many nights cuddling under starry skies. Mike and I were desperately in love (with the girls) and Carrie and Cassie left no doubt they were in lockstep with us. "Puppy love" fell far short of the powerful affection we held for the twins. "Kodiak Bear love" would be more accurate. It may not have the sustained endurance but is capable of incredible bursts of strength. Whatever the term, Mike and I were incapacitated. Maybe we did fit the "puppy love" definition in one respect. We would have followed these girls anywhere, an opportunity that would soon present itself.

We went right up to the wire — a couple days prior to the girls' departure — before we awoke to reality... *"For real, you guys are really going back home? Why? Do you have to?"* Indeed, we had been in complete denial. I believe to have consciously acknowledged the transient nature of our relationship would have prevented its existence altogether. Instead, we chose to live entirely "in the moment." Carrie was particularly devastated. She cried incessantly. It was not a show cry. It was bad. Like a woman crying for the loss of an only child. Mike was also in crisis. When he was down or depressed he became very quiet. He was normally quiet but when sad he became almost catatonic. I knew Mike well and was keenly aware of the signs of an impending episode. He would detach himself from reality and was in some remote "safe zone", far away from the threat. He could not be reached, seriously withdrawn and unresponsive to attempts to engage him in conversation. While Cassie and I were reacting with a more measured and normal expression of sadness, I worried Mike and Carrie might ultimately require some kind of psychotherapy!

Steeped in despair, we knew we had to devise a plan, somehow, to perpetuate our whirlwind romances. We frantically searched for possibilities and vowed neither money, time, nor distance could prevent our reunion. The answer came like a thunderbolt. OF COURSE! Mike and I would go to California. Wow! After all, wasn't that our dream to begin with? And now it came with a bonus of 2 beautiful beach girls? This was looking better all the time — not a tragedy at all! You know the adage, "When one door slams shut another one opens." Four thousand miles? Just a big open door! Incredible how these rare strokes of good fortune sometimes just drop right into your lap! The gorgeous twins were exactly what we needed to commit to our California dream —— almost like destiny!

Our gloom turned to joy as we busied ourselves making plans. Carrie's eyes dried up. Mike returned to the land of the living. The twins would fly out in a couple of days with mom and dad. Mike and I would follow — on foot! Carrie teased Mike and me with all the wonderful things that would await us in California. We would camp out in her garage. She had already cleared it with her parents. She and Cassie would make us great food. We would enjoy the California sun and Seal Beach. Experience the beautiful Pacific Ocean we had dreamed of! Mike and I were overwhelmed! We were also a little overwhelmed knowing the girls' plane would have them safely in L.A. in 6 hours while who knew when we would arrive and in what condition. Love would be our fuel. You know, the "I love you." "I love you, too." "I love you more." "No way, I love YOU more." Now keep in mind, days earlier we had been strangers. No mistaking that —"Kodiak Bear Love"! (or, as my friend Gennaro would say, "♫ When the moon hits your eye♪…")

Mike and I needed to prepare for the trip. Make plans but nothing too elaborate. We both intuitively felt getting to LA fast was far more important than fussing about details. Appropriate provisions such as enough food for the estimated length of the trip, a water canteen, toilet paper for the times we were stuck in between towns, and maybe a basic first aid kit, seemed like clutter. We would "travel light". One "detail" we did acknowledge was money. We had none! The notion of taking a temporary job was distasteful to both of us. We were not particularly lazy (I would say average lazy for our age) but a job would rob us of precious California vacation time with the twins. We had had jobs in the past — I more so than Mike. Actually, Mike had held one solitary job. I loved the country and had lived for a time on the farm. I would take on jobs for farmers, usually at rock bottom wages. The farmers were typically very thrifty and would work me like a mule. I was pretty tough though and usually impressed them with my tenacity. Mike's employment history was rather sad. Around age sixteen his mother had orchestrated his landing a job pumping gas at the Walcott Truckstop on I-80 just 10 miles away. She had spoiled Mike a little during his childhood and I believe she feared Mike's 18th birthday might come and go without the slightest influence on his pursuing a career. The comfort of home and mom's excellent sandwiches piled high with mayo would be hard to part with. Sadly, Mike's job had ended abruptly — before noon on his first day, immediately after he filled both tanks of an 18-wheel DIESEL truck with regular gasoline! No mercy, no forgiveness, no second chance. Mike quickly settled back into his unemployed status and I believe fortified his natural inclination that work was an inherently bad thing. I think he really wanted to forget the whole traumatic event, however, he had made the mistake of recounting the story to me. It spread like a fire which I regularly stoked. In all fairness, I should say Mike matured to be wholly devoted, talented, and hardworking during his career.

In the 1960s and '70s radical changes occurred in America's culture and mores: the Sexual Revolution, recreational drug use, the rock-and-roll obsession, and peace movements. Furthermore, hippies could indulge themselves in these lifestyles and at least make an attempt at dignity and respect by feigning themselves to be devoted ambassadors of "love" and "peace." Who can contend with love and peace? Or such was the hope. In any event, the nation's youth were going places they had never been before.

Mike and I also dabbled in the hippie movement, at least to some degree. Mike's hair touched the top of his shoulders. I don't know exactly where I stood. I suppose somewhere between Buck Owens and Alice Cooper. I identified with the hippies in terms of music and wanting total freedom but being a country boy at heart, I believe I had a little redneck in me as well. The long, long hair on men seemed strange to me (Though I gave my "best friend" a pass).

Of course, the typical hippie didn't work, however, was in sync with his working critics in the need and desire for money. The solution? Panhandling, or simply asking strangers for money. Mike and I also panhandled but on a very limited and emergency basis. I had a hard time dealing with the guilt and shame. I found it a little too humiliating. Many hippies did it with exuberance, without a hint of reservation. It was actually ironic. Hippies would berate the conformist and exploitive lives of these "plastic people" and then ask them to share the spoils. Also interesting was the common expression hippies used when referring to an unfortunate circumstance — "bummer", a modification of the derogatory term "bum" — meaning a person of low degree, averse to work, cleanliness or responsibility!

I was recently in San Francisco out on Fisherman's Wharf and saw a man in his late twenties mimicking a 1960s hippie. He was dressed in a tie dye T-shirt, long hair, tear drop sunglasses, and bandana, and flashing a big silly pot grin. The baby-boomer tourists loved him as he gave the peace sign. He held a placard that read "NEED CASH FOR WEED." When people pulled out their cameras, he would flip the sign over and it read "TWO DOLLAR PHOTO FEE." "Donations" filled the can he held. The scene was very reminiscent of the times when Mike and I journeyed to California.

I remember once when Mike and I lacked the money for admission to the Colosseum Ballroom in Davenport to see a rock band. We decided to embarrass ourselves and panhandle, also referred to as "spare-changing". We were obviously young, strong and able-bodied, so begging like a severely disabled person would seem preposterous. Regardless, the practice was commonplace. Mike decided to try his luck in front of the upscale Italian restaurant downtown. Most of the patrons were wealthy so it seemed like a good prospect. I chose a theater entrance several blocks away. Panhandlers couldn't cluster. One needed the appearance of a lone casualty of life. A group might appear to be a malingering bunch of hippies, like the Manson Clan.

How Mike sufficiently overcame his shyness to approach people in formal attire and ask for money, I have no idea. It was hard enough for me. He did fare well though. I believe his sheepish demeanor coupled with the big innocent eyes were excellent qualifications. I even wondered if some of his donors suspected they were helping someone who was mentally challenged. Our parents had no idea how we were generating cash!

The plan was to panhandle at the designated spots, then maybe wander, if need be, or if asked to vacate the premises — then meet at 6:45 sharp in front of the ballroom. I was there on time, admission money in hand, but Mike was a no-show. He finally arrived at around 8 o'clock, looking a little distressed.

"Where have you been?" I asked. "Did you get the money?"
"No," he muttered. "I didn't get the money and I think I'm gonna throw-up!"

Mike and I had eaten hamburgers and fries at "Sandys" just before panhandling and I wondered if he had gotten a bad burger.

"Do you think it was the food at "Sandys"?" I asked.

Jacob Sparks

"No, I was panhandling outside the restaurant and this rich guy with a suit on was going in. I asked for money and he wanted to know why I needed it. I didn't know what to say, so I told him I was hungry. He said, 'Come on, we'll take care of that!' He took me into the restaurant, got us a booth and ordered two spaghetti suppers with rolls, salad and milk. I had to eat the whole thing!"

It was one thing to accept money from a person and quickly move on. This situation was obviously very different — a worst case scenario. Neither Ronnie, Chad nor I would have *ever* sat down and eaten with a stranger, hungry or full, however Mike was too shy to refuse! I could vividly picture the event. Mike, nearly paralyzed with stage fright, sitting directly across from the benevolent gentleman, nearly nose to nose, as the man queried him as to what tragedies had led to his life on the streets at such an early age. Add to this torment Mike eating a large meal on a full stomach while pretending to be famished! Another story I would never let die.

As we watched the western sky swallow the twins' plane I think we both felt overwhelmed. Our strength and passion for what we intended to do disintegrated with the jet's contrail. Grim reality appeared in its place — by nightfall the girls we loved would be half a continent away!

Chapter 4
On the Road

We escaped our encounter with reality, unscathed. The next morning Mike and I awoke, totally recovered from the fears and sadness of the day before. Love-sickness was again in full command! We spent no more than an hour packing, at best. A couple pairs of "cut-offs", one pair of blue jeans, two pairs of socks, a long-sleeved shirt, and one T-shirt a piece. We took toothbrushes, toothpaste, a bar of soap, two wash cloths and hand towels, two sleeping bags — but somehow, no shampoo!

Mike's mom was a devout (and long-time) member of "Brand X" dieters. That was reflected in every cupboard of her kitchen and consequently dominated the food supply that went into our suitcase. We packed roughly 2 dozen miniature cans of diet soup, each 98% liquid with 2 teaspoons of carrots and celery, probably some salt substitute and a pinch of delicious lo-cal herbs (or roughly the nutritional equivalent of distilled water!) We also took one loaf of bread and a 16 oz. jar of peanut butter — thankfully! And money? We gleaned $6.50 out of Mike's room and called it good. Granted, $6.50 bought more in 1971 than it does today but was still an unrealistically small amount to fund such a long trip with so many uncertainties. $6.50 would be roughly the equivalent of $20 today.

In defense of our setting off with that ridiculous amount of cash (if there is one), were two things. One, in our amorous manias, we were seriously limited in the ability to utilize logic or consider problematic contingencies. In our simple and uncomplicated view, the trip to LA would be swift, taking little more time than had someone driven us straight through. We would be there in just a few days, probably three, worst case scenario four! We could get by on a few sandwiches and the diet food. Two, when we did arrive in LA, I would ask my mom to send money. I would have secured the money prior to our leaving but my parents had recently moved to Missouri and were 150 miles away. And, as I mentioned, our departure was of an urgent nature. Besides, we would have safe haven the moment we hit LA. We would be fine. We thumbed our noses at the prospect of hardships and adversity. It was like, "Bring it on, rough us up a little. It can only enhance our appearance, rugged, lean, and tanned, when the girls see us again!"

Mike kissed his mom and he and I jumped into my older brother's 1957 Chevy who would drive us the 10 miles to I-80. We begged him to go, too, but he was 6 years older than us and definitely not into the hippy thing. We loved each other and his final look toward me took me back to yesteryear and times when I was headed for trouble. This time he couldn't help. I was 17 and had my mind made up.

We looked good when we hit the interstate and headed west. I think all expeditioners look good at this point, fresh and strong with handsome smiles. Our unfounded sense of confidence was bolstered by a ride to Iowa City, some 50 miles away almost immediately. However, we sat stalled at the Hawk-I Truck Stop interchange there for hours. We took a break in the shade under the 1st Avenue bridge overpass.

"Hey Mike, you hungry?"

"Yeah," he answered, "but I don't want any soup."

"Me either," I said. "Why don't I go over to the truckstop and snag us a burger. You stay here with the stuff."

Now let's see — we're one fortieth of the way to L.A. and we spend one third of our trip fund… how did that go… one over forty equals x over… who had time for nonsense like that in school with the incredible abundance of girl and food options so readily accessible? Our excursion would remain budgetless, and soon, penniless!

As adults, traveling together on long trips can really strain a relationship. Seventeen-year-olds (actually Mike had just turned 18) are different. Full of naivety, love, patience, and foremostly, forgiveness. We had not yet learned to hold grudges. We could pout for brief periods but not embrace long-term resentment. Our hearts were big and soft. We forgave and forgot, remarkably fast. We had known each other for several years and although the closest of friends, our trip would bring us even closer. We walked and walked, for seemingly endless miles between rides. We talked about life (what little we knew about it) and our dreams of the future but mostly about Carrie and Cassie, California, and the Pacific Ocean.

If you think the Iowa landscape is boring, drive across Nebraska. You'll long for Iowa! But we weren't bored for long. For one thing the heat was oppressive. Nothing like the life-threatening heat we would experience later in the Mohave Desert, but still bad. Secondly and worse was the Nebraska state policy on hitchhikers. The state saw these hippie hitchhikers as nothing more than young flamboyant hobos who had a negative effect on the state. They provided no economic stimulus and should they be tolerated on the interstates or allowed to congregate in towns they could only have an adverse impact on tourism. I suspect Nebraska tourism could ill-afford adversity (all due respect to their stunning landscape).

We would soon experience, firsthand, the Nebraska Highway Patrol's zero tolerance for hitchhikers. Scare them, threaten them, force them off the interstate or take them to jail, seemed to be their policy. They were like Nazi SS guards, heartless and cruel. They wanted hippies to pass the word across the country: Don't come to Nebraska, go around it! We were not far into Nebraska when we had our first encounter with the NHP, roughly seventy miles west of Omaha. We were at the west end of a long string of hitchhikers, maybe a quarter mile long. As we peered back eastward towards oncoming traffic and the line of hippies, we saw a puzzling development. A state trooper was pulled over and hitchhikers were leaving the roadside, crossing the ditch, climbing the field fence and entering farmland. We had no idea what was occurring — until the officer eventually worked his way up to us. He gave the order:

"Get off the interstate! Get off the right-of-way (ditch)!"

"Where do you want us to go?" I asked.

"I don't care," he said. "Get off state property."

Again, I asked, "Where are we supposed to go?"

He answered, "Go across the fields to the next town."

"How far is the next town?" I asked.

"Twenty miles," he said. "If I catch you on the road when I come back you're going to jail!"

The patrolman was seriously dedicated. Although his visage commanded respect, it came more by way of fear than professionalism. I got the distinct impression he had been expressly groomed and designated as the "Hippie Enforcement Officer". It was clear, hippies were outside the class of citizens the patrol boasted "To Serve and Protect". We headed for the ditch to join the other travelers who

Jacob Sparks

were crossing the fence and walking in chest-high brush in 100° heat!

Under the surface of this seemingly simple scenario of a highway patrolman harassing hitchhikers lay a far more insidious societal dilemma. The hippie population was indeed massive and growing. Although they were a generally nonviolent group, they certainly brought no benefit to their host city or locale. Illicit drug use and promiscuous sex were by no means victimless or without consequence. The greater the hippie population, the greater the potential for collateral fallout, often demonstrated by large concerts, Woodstock being the granddaddy of them all. The police really didn't have a clue as how to resolve the problem. They didn't want to fill their jails with hippies. Feeding and housing hippies would only expand the burden. Not to mention relatives (more hippies?) might migrate to town to visit their incarcerated loved ones. Scaring and chasing them resolved little. The hippie population would continue to cross the state like a revolving door, making the irresistible trip to California and back.

Our fellow hitchhikers informed us these hardships were normal occurrences in life on the road. An occupational hazard. Most of them were older and seemed to take it in stride, whereas Mike and I were traumatized. We had only begun our long journey. How could we endure encounters like this for thousands of miles? The glamour and exhilarating freedom of being on the road to California vanished. The stability of home and family was replaced with fear and profound insecurity. It was not the love, flowers, pot and hippie comradery we had imagined. I realized more and more as our trip progressed, the true story of these hippie nomads — as opposed to the romanticized version. A comparison to the 1930's was striking. As popularized by John Steinbeck's, The Grapes of Wrath, the mass exodus of Americans westward, primarily with a California destination, had remarkable similarities to this hippie migration. Of course the Great Depression which began in 1929 bankrupted many families, leaving them without subsistence. Many lost their farms and/or homes. California offered hope as a place to find work, particularly "stoop labor" (picking vegetables). The hippie migration was far more recreational and by choice, though producing nearly identical hardships. Both groups of these wandering souls were indigent. Both hitchhiked or drove old vehicles of dubious reliability. We followed I-80 — they had followed the legendary "Route 66". Both hoped for redemption in the sunny refuge of California. Both were famous in the songs of their day. Many in both groups likely found their destination disappointing. Both groups, while missing their homes, would be shunned by society in general and ruthlessly dealt with by police. Destitute and weary, both groups, though decades apart, would find a common comfort in alcohol and drugs.

When the patrolman pulled away and was out of sight I yelled, "Come on Mike!" as I started back across the ditch to the interstate.

"Man, what are you doing?" Mike asked, in shock.

"We're not walking 20 miles in this heat! We don't even have any water,"' I replied. "Let's get down the road to that bridge, fast. One of us will hitchhike keeping a close eye on the road while the other hides under the bridge. We'll try to keep a low profile using the bridge for cover. Plus it will give us breaks in the shade. Maybe we can catch a ride before the trooper comes back."

Mike was adamantly opposed to my plan yet agreed hiking in the heat and bushes was a grim alternative, especially in cutoffs! We set our plan in motion. It was tense. I thumbed on the road, scanning the horizon for the trooper's car roof lights while Mike did his best to peer from his lower vantage point. It seemed like days and a thousand cars later (probably an hour) when lo and behold, a woman in the most typical hippie mode, in the most typical hippie van pulled over. She wore flowers in her hair. Painted flowers adorned her VW Van. She had stopped before picking us up and purchased a large bag of fresh Bing cherries. She donned a warm and welcoming smile on her face as we piled in the van. She passed the bag of cherries to us and they tasted absolutely heavenly. Like wary foxes, though, we only took a couple and thanked her before handing them back. We would maintain that posture for the remainder of the trip, careful not to offend, as we came to fully appreciate our frailty.

As the young woman pulled the van back on the road and got up to speed, I alerted Mike, "Check it out."

He looked out the back window and saw the frightening site. The state trooper was right behind us, following no further back than one car length! We both whipped around and faced the front of the van, only occasionally peeking back to see if he was signaling to pull us over. He knew we were in the van and had apparently been in close enough proximity to view us catching the ride. He also knew we beat him — that we had boldly defied his orders, unlike the others, and returned to the road! Thankfully, he obviously considered getting us out of his jurisdiction to be more important than satisfying his anger. He followed closely for a few miles, then sped away. We were safe with the little earth mother in the hippie van, but for how long? Sustained safety would prove to be increasingly elusive. I was beginning to realize wanderlust was for the stout-hearted and came at a price. I can still see their images in my mind. Those pathetic hitchhikers wading through the tall brush, glistening with sweat, as 6 foot saplings slapped them in their faces. They had been lured with tales and hopes of experiencing some sort of nirvana in the California Mecca. California, we later discovered, would demonstrate itself to be even more hippie hostile then Nebraska!

Songs encouraged young people to get out on the road. California was the favorite destination. The Haight-Ashbury district in San Francisco was enormously popular as was Greenwich Village in New York City. Popular music belied the facts. Songs such as the Eagles' 'Take It Easy': "Well, I'm standing on a corner in Winslow

Arizona and such a fine sight to see. It's a girl my Lord, in a flatbed Ford, slowing down to take a look at me…."

OR

Janis Joplin's 'Me and Bobby McGee': "Busted flat in Baton Rouge, headed for the train, feeling nearly faded as my jeans. Bobby thumbed a diesel down just before it rained. Rode us all the way to New Orleans…."

The music of the day was a powerful influence on young people, glamorizing this bum-life, essentially leading adolescents nowhere, with no redeeming outcome at all. In fact, many times quite the opposite in terms of jail, drug addiction and overdose, and the consequences of indiscriminate sex and unwanted pregnancies. I don't mean to disparage these kids, I was one of them. Like lambs, most were simply looking for happiness and some place to belong, a purpose, and foremostly, something to believe in.

When we pulled away in the VW Van I felt a sense of sadness to leave the others behind. The trooper had meant business. He *was* coming back, forcing the transients to continue the hard trek through the brush into the night. I also realize, looking back, that many of these poor souls in the weeds had some serious war stories — such as the one Mike and I was just beginning.

While both of us had a commendable degree of empathy for these people, as the days and hardships mounted, we also saw a sinister trait developing in ourselves. Desperation became a common part of our daily lives and we began to adapt to it. Our youthful innocence would soon be compromised.

Chapter 5
Nebraska Exodus

Of all the spectacular sights Mike and I were to lay our eyes on — the Tahoe area, Reno at midnight, the Rockies — I believe the "WELCOME TO WYOMING" sign would rank among the best. Our several days in Nebraska had seemed like weeks! The initiation into this travel club had indeed been rough. Catching a couple hours sleep here and there, in the trees behind a rest area on the interstate or under a bridge. One strategy we used was distancing ourselves far from other hitchhikers. We would also thumb rides at night when the NHP were less present — unfortunately so were the rides! Additionally, people were more hesitant to offer rides in the dark. All this on starvation rations and only infrequent access to water at gas stations!

One of my brothers, who had joined the Marines years earlier, told scary stories about his boot camp training. I thought, it couldn't be any worse than this! But, like Marine recruits, the resilience of healthy 17 and 18 year olds is amazing. Despite the arduous nature of the trip, our spirits would come up for air. Our hearts longed for Carrie and Cassie but another topic that rivaled for equal time was the prospect of seeing, touching, smelling, and swimming in the Pacific. Remember, we were Iowans, located about as far from a beautiful ocean as one can get in our country. Lewis' Lake was cool, but really only a puddle — not a wave to be found. We had heard a little about California beaches and of course had seen them in movies. We wondered how big the waves were. Could you surf the water off the LA Coast? Could we rent surfboards (once our funds were replenished)?

For a moment I let my imagination go. There we were, in all our splendor, riding a monster wave with maximum agility, Mike's arms extended for balance as his hair blew back, his body tanned and chiseled while he sported a confident smile. I was right there beside him doing some cool maneuvers, certainly for a novice. And, of course, Carrie and Cassie peering on in beautiful swimsuits from their perch on the white sand. Granted, though that scenario was not plausible, I knew one thing that was: we would have some awesome stories to tell back in Iowa. Our mediocre status would never be the same. Our small group of friends had never been out of the state. California and the Pacific Ocean were like Rio to us. We would take everything we could get off the beach that wasn't nailed down. Sand, sea shells, driftwood — everything we could carry in our bags — as souvenirs and proof!

We finally reached North Platte, Nebraska. We were beginning to believe we would be permanent "outlaws" in the state. Out of peanut butter at this point, there were still over 1,500 miles to go to reach LA! Had we enough brain activity to thoroughly fathom our predicament we would have probably *surrendered* to the police in hopes they would ship us home. We did, however, come to understand we were in trouble. Our growing hunger was a constant reminder.

A newer SUV went by. I believe it was a Chevrolet Suburban.

"Hey!" Mike yelled.

"Hey, what?" I asked.

"Come on, man, they're stopping!" he replied.

Aside from police, rides were hard to come by in Nebraska. We ran as fast as possible carrying a big suitcase and backpack. Occasionally, a vehicle would pull over, typically far past our position, as though they were stopping for us. After running several hundred yards with our vagabond luggage, the car would speed away with the occupants shouting obscenities or making offensive gestures. This was a particularly disheartening event for the hitchhiker who (at least Mike and me) were already struggling with the rigors of the road. The Suburban, thankfully, offered no such cruel surprises. We piled in and introduced ourselves. We exchanged our stories, where we were from and our destinations. These two young men (early 20's) were cordial and such a relief from what we had been experiencing. They were headed for Alaska on a wilderness adventure. Sounded cool but paled, we thought, as compared to where we were going and who was waiting for us. The van was comfortable and even though we were hungry we were overjoyed at our good fortune. Moreover, the men would take us all the way to Cheyenne, Wyoming! Our hosts would liberate us. They were apparently well-financed as evidenced by the Suburban, and also all the lavish supplies it contained. It looked like overkill, albeit we had no idea as to the projected length of their excursion (nor did we have any concept of realistic trip planning!). Everything aboard was new. Fishing gear, camping gear, bush attire, boots, guns, and food — lots and lots of food. It was punishing to be so hungry and travel for hours amidst boxes of sardines, Dinty Moore stew (real soup!), chips and cookies. Still, our foremost concern was getting to LA as soon as possible. Sociologists tell us man's number one primal priority is food. That is, before romance, shelter or any other form of self-preservation. Teenage boys in love were obviously not included in that study!

We enjoyed the security of being in such a luxury van with normal and friendly escorts. We could now sleep without fear of strangers, the NHP, or the elements. A wonderful shelter in this storm. As we left Nebraska our moods were improving. Our dread of the NHP left, though we had no idea what hitchhiking laws in subsequent states would be like. For now we were two happy vagrants, traveling first class!

Wyoming spread out before us with a topography that was altogether new and strange. Granted, the land was somewhat dusty and barren but this was our first view of mountains and even if not Mount Hood, we were dazzled. Our driver decided to stop at a rest area for a nap. He and his friend were tired. Not so much with Mike and me.

Jacob Sparks

We had a newfound sense of hope and our vigor had returned despite our continued fast. We got out of the Suburban and aimlessly wandered the area. I had a large, fast-growing plantar's wart on the bottom of my right foot. I had no idea what it was, however the pain was exquisite. It was difficult to stand or walk, sadly, nearly all we did during our waking hours. Given the right motivation, however, I could run like a rabbit. I was very fit and an excellent runner (for short distances), swimmer, and wrestler. I also had exceptional upper body strength. In high school, our coach would extract me from my regular classroom and take me down to the gym to demonstrate climbing the rope. The rope was one and a half inches in diameter and attached to the ceiling. The objective, of course, was to climb the rope to the ceiling and descend back to the floor. I performed the feat in a unique manner that impressed the coach. That was, to flip my feet up toward the ceiling placing each foot on either side of the rope with my legs extended in a straight plane. I was upside down and used my feet only to guide me, doing all the climbing with my arms —— clear to the ceiling and back down while maintaining the inverted position. An adult might have considered it to be a ridiculous thing to do and wonder: Why? The odd nature of the stunt, I felt, was easily overwhelmed by the fact no one else at the school could duplicate it. "Uniquely cool" was my teenage perspective of the performance!

Mike and I quickly spotted the mountain behind the rest area bathroom facility. We were captivated. "Let's climb it," Mike said and we both broke into a run. We had assumed climbing the mountain would be similar to climbing a hill back in Iowa, only with a way better view. After approximately 15 minutes of exhaustive work and no appreciable progress towards the summit we realized our foolishness and returned to the Suburban.

We didn't have to travel far in Wyoming before Cheyenne came into view. We had mixed feelings. We were extremely happy to have been freed from Nebraska yet knew that Cheyenne was the end of the line as far as our luxury ride. We would soon be out on the road again with all the associated dangers. Our hunger grew as it had been to 2 or 3 days since we had eaten. It got to the point where food was all we could think about. Our driver and his partner decided to stop at a diner on the interstate before entering the Cheyenne area traffic. Mike and I waited in the Suburban. Sumptuous, mouth-watering restaurant smells wafted into the Suburban as our hosts exited the vehicle. As they turned the corner of the building and headed for the door of the cafe I told Mike, "Keep watch and tell me if they come back." "Why?" Mike asked. "Never mind Mike, just do it," I replied. Earlier I had seen a big jar of peanut butter in one of the boxes when the driver had been searching for a map. Peanut butter was a particularly precious food for the road because of its nonperishable quality. "You can't do that, get out of there!" Mike hollered. "Be quiet Mike!" I whispered as I removed the jar and slid it down into Mike's backpack and clasped it shut. Mike's big eyes were glaring at me with strong disapproval. For a moment he resembled the highway patrolman back in Nebraska. "We have to, Mike," I reasoned. "We've got one dollar and we can't go on forever not eating!" Mike seemed to calm down and the Alaska-bound men soon returned. Mike and I talked later about what we (actually I) had done. We agreed we would rather not have stolen from these guys — after all, they had rescued us from Nebraska. On the other hand, we were in a desperate situation. At Cheyenne the men were to take I-25 north and Mike and I would continue on I-80 west. We said our goodbyes and wished each other well.

Mike and I looked towards the truck stop. "Let's go get some bread and chow-down," I said. Contrary to his earlier chastisement, Mike now offered no objection. What did surprise me, though, was that within one hour we (actually me again) would perpetrate another theft that was way worse!

Chapter 6
Beth and Linda

Mike and I sat on the curb at the side of the truck stop and unceremoniously prepared our first meal in days. Truly a hobo feast. Any dignity or integrity that we left Iowa with was seriously compromised in the trek across Nebraska. In mere days we had descended to the lowest echelons of society and, just as remarkably, seemed okay with it. I spread the stolen peanut butter like a chef, liberally, in celebration of our ill-gotten bounty. Although neither of us was proud of how we had acquired the peanut butter, it was not reflected at all in our appetites as we devoured the perfect meal to break a fast — no drinks and multiple sandwiches of snow-white bread with gobs of peanut butter!

Our dramatic shift in behavior had striking similarities to a Snoopy movie I had seen. Snoopy was living large, extremely overindulged in leisure. He whiled away his hours in self-pleasures. No chores, no responsibilities, and no cares. One afternoon found him, in typical form, lying on his back eating his favorite pizza on top of his doghouse. A post-meal doze transported him to a completely new and threatening environment — the untamed Alaskan tundra. The weather was bitterly cold with a blizzard underway. He was alone and totally defenseless. His wild canine instincts were stunted (Beaglehood), and prospects for survival were slim. Snoopy ultimately located a pack of wild and ferocious wolves. He knew his only hope lay in joining the pack. His introduction into the group was scary and filled with challenges and danger. He assumed the rank of lowest subordinate but by winter's end had risen to the alpha position with pack members approaching him with the highest degree of caution and respect. Rather quickly, Snoopy had learned to "man-up" (or "wolf-up") and acclimate to his harsh surroundings. It was a hilarious movie, yet, in many respects, paralleled our experience on the road. The post-dream Snoopy had changed dramatically. He now had a deep appreciation for his owners and accommodations.

As we finished our meal we saw an old, late 1950s pickup truck pull into the parking lot. Like street people, we were developing the habit of taking notice of everything in our environment — every detail. As I mentioned, Mike and I were adapting. We had always been extremely laid back, almost to the point of being dull. I would guess our blood pressure must have averaged around 80/40. But that was changing fast. Our life in the slow lane was gone. We were becoming constantly observant of our surroundings, watchful for opportunities — or threats! The pickup held two young women around 20 years old in the cab and in the small bed of the truck were two young men about our age, maybe a year or two younger. The boys had longer hair and generally resembled Mike and me. They had that distinct road-worn look. Also, because of their age, we reasoned they were not girlfriends and boyfriends but rather the boys were likely hitchhikers.

From our seat on the curb we watched the pickup and its occupants. The girls exited the truck and went inside the restaurant to eat. Curiosity ultimately prevailed and we sauntered over to the pickup and offered a casual greeting. The boys were younger than us and a little more naïve, (if that was possible). They quickly divulged they too (along with everyone else in North America) were destined for California. I'm sure they were both minors and that, we had learned in our life-on-the-road experience, had the potential to become a serious ordeal. Police would stop, harass and sometimes arrest hitchhikers, many times holding them briefly and then release them. If, however, the person was a minor, it violated most states laws to simply release them back onto the streets. Police were technically obligated to hold these youths, releasing them only to parents, guardians or another state agency. I would not turn 18 until late fall and that, in all likelihood, was beyond the timeframe of our trip — a contingency that could spell trouble. The two boys disclosed all their plans and good fortunes: their departure and destination spots and how they had luckily connected with these girls at a truck stop back east. Most importantly, they informed us the girls were going all the way to San Francisco where they were to meet their boyfriends who were service members stationed there. The boys were aware of no threat by sharing this information with us and at the time neither were we. None of us were cognizant of the dramatic changes both our itineraries would take in the next several minutes.

Beth and Linda

The girls leisurely ate their meals in the restaurant. The young men fidgeted and asked us, if the girls returned, to tell them they would be right back. They grabbed their bags and proceeded to the station to make a bathroom visit. Before they left, they suggested we might ask the girls if we too could ride along.

The girls returned in their absence and Mike and I quickly introduced ourselves and let them know we were also destined for California, hitchhiking. They immediately asked if we had drivers' licenses. I said yes, Mike said no — although he indeed had one. One of the girls asked if we had seen two guys who had been traveling with them. "Yes," I said. She asked where they were, to which I replied, "I think they got a ride." The girls invited us to join them on their journey to California. We quickly loaded up and were off!

There is no justifying what I had done. The peanut butter was one thing — we were starving and the Alaska-bound men had plenty. It was wrong for sure but one could rationalize. As we set off on this last leg of the journey to California with our new lady friends, I frequently reflected on what was sacrificed and what was stolen to provide the transportation. In effect we took the boys' tickets they had been so proud of and were even willing to share! The deception was heartless and cruel. I told myself I had done it "spur of the moment" and there was some truth to that. But I also had a strong sense these girls were focused more on finding someone who could legally share the driving than on how many boys they could pile in the truck. I knew I could influence their decision with my comment. In any event, it was awful!

Beth and Linda were fun and spirited though very careful and calculating. The girls kept their hair up (in buns) and covered with bandanas, the reason for which we would later discover. We made a great foursome and drove west with an unbridled enthusiasm, both for our destination and the joy we might find in the journey.

We quickly learned the pickup was indeed old and in poor condition.

The girls, desperate to unite with their boyfriends, had been strictly instructed not to drive over 40 mph, advice they carefully abided by. The number 40 had become almost a phobia to the girls, so much so they preferred, to be absolutely safe, to stay a few miles per hour below 40. The problem that posed, of course, was a certainty of traffic tickets for driving under the minimum speed of 40 mph. The girls had found someone with a license, desperate enough to drive 37 or 38 mph. Me! Mike could have driven as well. He had a valid driver's license but after telling the girls he didn't, I couldn't convince them otherwise. Mike had a dry sense of humor and would often say things that only he appreciated the comic element of. The girls, on the other hand, were focused, no-nonsense, and on a mission. They didn't think things were ringing up right and were taking no chances. Why would someone say he had no driver's license when he did? They could see maybe someone saying he had one when he didn't. Seemed strange to them and they declared he was DEFINITELY not driving. Mike loved the stir he had caused. I demanded he show his license to them. He refused and calmly asserted, "I don't have one." I had to drop it as the girls were both beginning to think we were acting odd. Consequently, I was stuck behind the wheel continually as traffic tickets, all in my name, began to pile up on the dash. Despite creeping down the interstate at 30-some miles per hour, looking like hillbillies in a pickup that made people laugh as they passed, we were elated. And yes, EVERYONE passed! But it didn't matter. We had a 5 pound jar of peanut butter (chunky), a loaf of bread (and enough money for another one), two pretty companions, and a one-way ticket to San Francisco, where we would turn south to LA. "California, here we come…"

Beth and Linda were from the eastern U.S. and, like Mike and me, were in awe at all the new geographical sites that came into view. The cab of the pickup was small, and in addition to three of us, also held some of the more vital weather- sensitive belongings of the girls. We were packed in the cab as I drove nearly the entire

Beth and Linda

time. The girls were merciless when it came to that. Ordinarily, as a normal 17-year-old, I would have thought it cruel and unusual punishment to be forced to drive an ancient, ugly pickup down the interstate at 37 mph in broad daylight. We were conspicuously disgraced, but would thoroughly enjoy the next few days with these girls, regardless. The men in the suburban had rescued us from Nebraska, now Linda and Beth would spirit us to California! The future couldn't seem brighter! I would drive up to 12 hours a day at 38 mph, constantly looking for the next set of red flashing lights. Occasionally I would wonder just what consequences all of these tickets on the dash might hold for me. I feared there would be a reckoning in the future. They did appear very official and I believe had some threatening words in small print on the back should someone be foolish enough to ignore their authority. Would the next highway patrolman inform me I had just exceeded the maximum number of unanswered tickets and arrest me on the spot? Would the police have my house staked out when I returned home? I seriously began to worry about it!

The girls were desperate to get to San Francisco as soon as possible. The trip was taking longer than planned. Their arrival had to coincide with their boyfriends leaves of absence. Consequently they pushed me to drive longer hours. I didn't mind that as I had the same excitement in my heart for Carrie. To have a ride secured for days and hundreds of miles was invaluable, even at 38 miles an hour! Much better than hopscotching our way across states in 10-20 mile increments with hours-long periods of standing or walking. We were also police-proof while traveling with the girls.

As I've mentioned, the pickup was in poor condition. It had no windshield rear view mirror, only a side mirror which hung precariously from the driver's door. The fastidious highway patrol would always spot the deficiency but could not cite us for it as the infraction, albeit substandard, technically qualified as legal. Mike usually rode in the bed of the truck. I couldn't easily see the traffic behind us and had to repeatedly turn and look out the back glass for police. I typically saw only Mike's face, large and smiling, as he came close into my view. He was smiling, of course, about the stunt he had pulled off. Acting a little slow-witted and stating with a pitiful, yet earnest look on his face that he had no driver's license!

After, say, my 25th traffic ticket for going a measly 1 or 2 mph below the speed limit, I had to wonder if the United States had a crime priority conflict. Our country was experiencing exploding illegal drug trafficking, anti-war protests wreaking havoc at colleges, various "liberation" groups bombing public places and yet I have half the nation's police force pursuing me for driving 38 mph!

Mike and I bonded strongly on our adventure. Mike's sense of humor had always been excellent, though largely shrouded by his shyness. On the excursion to California I saw glimpses of a latent nature. In the ensuing years Mike would progressively transform into a gregarious and hilariously funny man. Almost constantly joking and very witty with a magnetic personality. A "good time Charlie." A "life of the party" kind of guy. I would never have anticipated the change.

At a gas station pit stop, Mike and I lamented the deplorable condition of our hair as we gazed in the bathroom mirror. How we had overlooked bringing along our shampoo was a mystery (and a tragedy). In the 1960s and '70s, natural, long, shiny hair was in vogue. Shampoo to this period was what hair cream was to the 1950's. Young people spent hours talking about which shampoo was the best. For teenagers, like Mike and me, to have dirty, dull, greasy hair was shameful. You could be a bum in every other respect: no job, no college, begging money, etc., but to have unattractive hair was inexcusable. It had been days since we had washed our hair and it was obvious. We would take sponge baths in gas station bathrooms — another scary dilemma in itself — but our hair situation went unresolved. We had a problem. We had no shampoo!

We continued our exciting tour through the western United States, in wonder. Salt Lake City was kind of cool to see. Spectacular mountains cradled the city like the hands of a loving giant.

Immediately beyond Salt Lake City was the Great Salt Lake. We were all excited to stop and check it out. Nothing particularly notable there (flat and barren terrain for miles) with the exception of two things. One, Linda and Beth bought a big bag of salt water taffy which they shared with us. It was so good to eat something besides peanut butter and bread. Two, there was water, lots of water. Mike and I, wearing cutoffs and no shirts, had a plan — an extremely dumb one that would have consequences. Although no one, absolutely no one, was out wading in the lake's acrid and caustic brew, Mike and I took it to be similar to the fresh water back home at Lewis' Lake. This, we reasoned, would be our long overdue opportunity to "freshen up" with a dip. I am certain, looking back, we were center stage as we began our casual walk into the lake in search of deep water we could swim in. I'm also confident normal, intelligent people were amused as Mike and I performed, like clowns before the circus crowd!

Our hope was that thoroughly drenching our bodies — and particularly our hair in the lake would have some kind of cleansing and refreshing effect even in the absence of shampoo. We had walked hundreds of yards and still the water was below our knees. It became apparent there was no deep water in this lake. We discussed it and on the count of three both dove into the shallow water. The effect was immediate and devastating! The water, like acid, filled our eyes even though they were closed. The burning was excruciating! I don't know if it was the heavy concentration of the salt alone or other minerals or chemicals that caused the intense fire-like pain (they make taffy out of this stuff?). We jumped to our feet and realized the stupidity of our action. We shamefully returned to shore with red eyes and a thick layer of brine on our bodies and hair. A sad decline from my glory days at Lewis' Lake! Linda and Beth enjoyed the performance appearing as older and wiser onlookers that would, of course, have known better.

In the days that followed our hair no longer blew in the breeze, despite the wind's velocity. It gathered itself in a few heavy clumps, surrendering totally to gravity and resisting our combs like asphalt!

As we studied our maps Mike and I realized San Francisco might not be in our future. Although the iconic "City by the Bay" had powerful appeal, our desperation to see the twins easily won the contest. The trip to L.A. looked quicker if we turned South at Sacramento on I-5.

I-80 west across Nevada was the long and winding road. I drove, pedal-to-metal up mountains and rode the brakes on the descent. As we neared the great and mighty California, we agreed to ignore both time and darkness to make entry into the state before we slept. I had been driving continuously for about 14 or 15 hours and asked Linda if she would give me a break. Mike and I rode in the bed of the truck as we entered Reno and all four of us were immediately children seeing a fully lit Christmas tree for the first time! I could see the girls' heads snapping this way and that to catch all the sights. Mike and I did the same in the back while making a midnight snack of, (drum roll please), peanut butter sandwiches!

This had to be the most extreme scene of non-conforming and odd combinations. The lights of the strip were like monstrous LED flood lights on steroids. Despite being midnight (or perhaps because of it) the streets bustled with all sorts of activity. Music playing, people drinking and heading into casinos, and hookers plying their trade, all in this carnival-like world. The flashing and intensely artificial neon lights made everything seem surreal. By contrast, there we were in an old farm truck. Hayseeds from back east, gawking at the sites while the girls tried to read their map and Mike and I spread peanut butter, like the Waltons took a wrong turn!

As we left Reno, we knew the California state line was close. Linda put me back behind the wheel and at the border we were stopped and checked for plants or vegetables on board. The concern, of course, was to not introduce exotic insects or plant diseases into this heavily-farmed state. We made it through and when we were out of sight of the border security check post, we let it go. Hurrahs, woo-hoos, laughing, shouting and screaming, "We made it!"

And then, as quickly and spontaneously as the joy had come, it vanished! Everyone became as silent and still as tombstones. It was strange and ominous —a foreboding sadness seemed to settle on all four of us.

Chapter 7
California —at Last

A short distance into California Beth asked me to turn on the dome light. I asked if something was wrong and she explained she wanted to check her map. As is the case with women (you could say things like this in 1971), and particularly Beth and Linda; every detail of the girls' trip was meticulously planned and executed. Beth told me to take the next exit and turn south on Highway 89. She didn't disclose why we were diverting off I-80 and I had learned to comply without questions. We drove a short distance to a rest area Beth had designated and I let the detour remain a mystery. We were all exhausted from the unusually long drive that day and resorted to preparing for sleep in the moonlit night.

Next morning we awoke to the most awesome sight! Beth and Linda had brought us to a bluff overlooking a meadow. The view was incredible! The surrounding mountains were replete with gorgeous pines towering over 100 feet tall, contrasting a vivid, blue, cloudless sky. "Come here!" Mike called to me as he stood peering over a guard rail a short distance away. He had that excited "kid look" he got when he had found something really cool. I joined him and gazed down to see the breathtaking Lake Tahoe!

The girls, just a couple years older than us, had been mature enough to plan and drive straight to this paradise. Our respect for them was definitely elevated. Soon we would have cause to be further impressed. Before leaving for Sacramento both girls took their bandanas off, releasing their hair. It was not your average, garden-variety hair. Their hair was big, full, luxurious, and long. What really baffled Mike and me was it's clean, healthy, and shiny condition. How could this be after all these days on the road? What was the magic of these bandanas? What were they made of? Most importantly, where could we get some? I think the girls really enjoyed showing off their hair. San Francisco was still a few hours away and it would have made more sense to have waited until they were closer to their boyfriends for the unveiling. The girls were pretty and their hair was stunning — indeed a humbling experience for Mike and me as we peered on in admiration through heavy dreadlocks that used to be hair — like theirs!

Our arrival in Sacramento was immediately disastrous. I believe the short-lived reward of double-crossing the boys and stealing from the men in the Suburban had run out and the consequences of our deal with the Devil had arrived. It was at this point the girls would continue west on I-80 while Mike and I turned south towards LA. Adversities would manifest in rapid succession. We had no sooner pulled over and stopped on the shoulder of the interstate when a California highway patrolman pulled up on our bumper, lights flashing. Mike and I had said our good-byes to the girls and were climbing out of the pick-up. The officer, of course, quickly recognized the "hippie hitchhiker scenario" and consequently we were marked men. "If that truck doesn't have a blown motor, you're going to jail," was the patrolman's greeting to me. Such a contrast to the Lake Tahoe welcome.

"Sorry, sir," I said, my words teaming with respect. "See, Beth and Linda, the girls who gave us a ride, are going on to San Fran —"

"I don't care where they're going. You're going to jail," the patrolman barked. "You don't stop on California interstates unless your vehicle is disabled!"

Mike and I followed the patrolman's orders, were handcuffed and placed in the backseat of his cruiser. I had made it so close to Carrie and now, almost certainly, I would be held in some jail until my parents somehow rescued me, or I turned eighteen. I was thoroughly depressed. I continued to plead with the officer, explaining we had been completely unaware of the law we had violated. I tried to placate him with assurances we would have never done so intentionally nor would we ever repeat the infraction. He was steadfast — there would be no mercy. We continued the unexpected tour of Sacramento streets as we stared blankly out our windows in forlorn silence. Abruptly the patrolman pulled over, let us out of the car, removed our handcuffs and with a mild reprimand let us go! We were in shock! Just what had caused the sudden shift in the officer's attitude was a mystery . . . LA was back on our itinerary!

We took up a hitchhiking position on the road and were giving cheers and hoorays, celebrating our release from custody and arrival to California. We were on the last leg of our journey, like the home stretch of a marathon.

Less than four hundred miles to relief: real food, beautiful girls and the Pacific Ocean! In our jubilation, Mike swung his backpack in several revolutions from his feet to the sky and let it go. It traveled upward approximately 20 feet and when it landed on the pavement we heard a muffled crunch sound, sort of like the chiropractor cracking your back! We looked at each other in horror, knowing exactly what had happened. The glass jar of peanut butter, our only food supply, was gone! We might have 2 or 3 days before we reached the girls, depending on rides and police encounters. We opened the backpack to see a peanut butter/glass paste stuck to our clothes and the meager belongings inside. A double bummer! We spent two hours sitting there on the ground trying desperately to clean and salvage what we could, all in the blazing sun.

We maintained excellent spirits despite the police greeting and peanut butter fiasco. We were so close to our destination and the road had been so long. Only occasionally would we touch on the topic of the inevitable return trip to Iowa. Kind of like two climbers 300 yards from the Everest Summit and one asks the other if he wants to do it again! The girls and Seal Beach were far more appealing topics than the trip home. We laughed, joked and spoke French! I had completed three years of French in school and was bursting at the seams with the language. Mike was not exactly the world traveler type but my choice for a protégé was limited. Regardless, he enthusiastically accepted the role and picked up the language quickly. Mike had never found his niche in school. He wasn't a dunce — he was clever and witty — but really, as far as one could get from the studious, scholarly type. For instance, we were continually barefoot in the summer months; however Mike reliably wore boots at all other times of the year. Kind of a Harley Davidson type guy, albeit a shy one. I would have thought Mike to be a terrible choice for foreign language but not so. His failure to connect in school, I believe, had left a void, a feeling of inadequacy. I think learning French provided the ego-boost he needed. I wondered if maybe he was imagining himself with some beautiful and highly refined lady in an upscale restaurant, delicately correcting the waiter's pronunciation of the French choices on the desert tray! Whatever the case, Mike was giving it the old college (Notre Dame?) try. I was impressed with his uninhibited willingness to emphatically infuse the proper enunciation with all the odd French sounds. He showed no reluctance to form his mouth in dramatic fashion, creating the throaty, almost choking sounds or the strong nasal emphasis. Those sounds most American students gave an English modification to avoid embarrassment amidst their school peers. Of course, I was the only "peer" and Mike was quite comfortable with me. He would exaggerate the French dialect and supplement it with all manner of head, hand, and arm gestures such as connecting all his fingertips on one hand and touching them to his lips as he spoke ("fingertip kiss"). Mike, mon ami, je t'aime! — Mike, my friend, I love you!

We were glad to leave Sacramento but realized the cities ahead would likely be similar. We now knew police contempt for long-haired hitchhikers seemed to uniformly prevail across the entire country. California was no exception and quite possibly worse due to its popularity as an end point destination and gathering spot for this nomadic tribe. I'm sure the CHP wanted these people to do a U-turn and head back east. But we were indeed on the home stretch and nothing short of a jail cell could dampen our spirits. I had no pictures of Carrie nor did I need any. She was so pretty and I could visualize every detail of her face. I could hear the allure in her soft and feminine voice. I also had total recall of every charming nuance she possessed. In just a few hours I would hold her again. Life just couldn't get any cooler than this!

California people seemed more affluent than those in previous states and consequently more reluctant to offer rides to shabby hitchhikers such as ourselves. Our hair was becoming more atrocious with each passing day. We really couldn't palpate our scalps any longer with our fingers. I worried what we might find when we could. Would it be like the rescued Border Collie with the matted coat? Hard telling what kind of pathological condition might be thriving there. We had stopped any attempts with our combs long ago!

Our rides were infrequent and as a result we did a lot of walking. The plantar's wart on my foot was particularly painful when there was no distraction. During times of minimal conversation the foot pain was front and center. At this point, however, nothing could trump our adrenalin. We were on the home-stretch. Only a couple hundred miles. We were battle-hardy and could belly-crawl that far!

We were seeing signs for towns we had heard of: Stockton, Fresno, and headed towards Bakersfield. Not necessarily distinguished cities among Californians but definitely a big deal for Mike and me. Our first day of travel in the state had not yielded much, less than 150 miles. As was our routine, we searched for a rest area with the required accommodations. There had to be trees and preferably lots of them. Even better was adjoining land with trees. If we could utilize such an area we were on private property and less likely to be harassed by the highway patrol. If we set up in a rest area with only a few isolated trees or bushes, we were far more conspicuous. The problem we faced was the route to LA followed the San Joaquin Valley (vegetable farms). California's status of being the "nation's salad bowl" was of no benefit to us, neither for cover nor food.

Our first night's sleep in California brought no unexpected surprises and the following morning was invigorating. The sun, the blue sky, the road ahead and of course our destination grew closer with each step. We had long debates regarding whether to walk or stand. Walking seemed to me to be of no advantage. The distance you covered in an hour by walking was overwhelmed in minutes with the next ride. Still, it was incredibly boring for teenagers to stand, sometimes for hours, in one spot. The heavy luggage was the other consideration. When we walked we had to lug the bags. Lots of factors — hence the long debates.

We caught a ride just north of Fresno around two in the afternoon. The man who picked us up was the conventional "traveling salesman". Fortunately, he had children approximately our age and felt a fatherly sense of compassion for us. He had been on the road since very early that morning and we were dismayed to find he planned on getting a room in Visalia, only thirty miles further down the road. This cloud, however, had a silver lining. When we related how arduous our journey had been, including the funny story of our "swim" in the Great Salt Lake and its residual effect on our hair, he made a generous and welcomed offer. Would we like to share his room in the motel overnight? Wow! We wanted to continue our advance southward, being so close to the girls, yet this offer was hard to resist. A bed, a bath, shampoo samples, and possibly an opportunity to wash our clothes! How in the world could we refuse?

The motel was a high-end one and the amenities overwhelmed us. Soon after checking in, our host resorted to a siesta in one of the queen-sized beds.

Psychologists say "regression" is defined as mentally returning to an earlier and more secure time of one's life. Mike and I became "thing one" and "thing two", like a couple of eleven-year-old cousins out on a road trip with uncle Larry! Life had been too grim, too long. The cathartic effect was powerful. We began restoring all our deficiencies (with the exception of food). We were ecstatic, running up and down the halls, checking out the grounds and swimming in the pool. We found the establishment's laundry machines and quickly utilized them, albeit with no detergent. Most notably we took turns in the shower. Thankfully, shampoo samples were abundant and I believe it was about the fourth or fifth shampoo/rinse repetition that we actually started seeing something that resembled lather. Remarkably, our scalps somehow seemed to have survived the chemical treatment with no residual damage. The bliss of the shower could only be matched by the bed, beautiful white sheets and numerous pillows. Our fellow hitchhikers would be skeptical of this tale as we exchanged stories out on the road. We would not forget nor re-experience the comforts and security of this night for some time.

The next morning we were off and with the exception of hunger were in excellent spirits. Clean bodies, clean clothes, and finally, *clean hair*! The salesman's route would divert him off the main thoroughfare within a few miles and we reluctantly said our goodbyes. We still had a couple hundred miles to LA but took an oath to make it yet that day. Our second day of no food had certainly not escaped our attention, but that was okay. In just hours we would feast like kings!

Chapter 8
LA, Treachery and Silver

LA was huge and daunting for two boys from "small town" Iowa. Everything moved so fast! The freeways easily lived up to their reputation. We hung onto a city map we had procured but it provided limited comfort. What we were seeing as we peered, wide-eyed, through the car windows, easily overwhelmed the security blanket effect of the map. Our driver assured us he would be dropping us off in a good spot relative to where he was going and where Carrie and Cassie lived. Thoughts of the twins had brought us through tremendously difficult times on the road and those same thoughts now tempered the anxieties the views of this monster city were generating.

Our driver pulled over and stopped. We thanked him and climbed out of the vehicle with an immediate sense of apprehension at what we saw. The neighborhood looked rough with old vacant buildings and poorly maintained row houses. We were comforted though, when we spotted two things. One, a phone booth to call the girls from. We knew they would rush to our rescue. Two, a McDonalds's restaurant was situated not far from the phone booth. We had desperately held onto enough change to provide a meager meal before either making it to the twins — or dying!

We had barely exited the car when a man, who looked deranged, yelled from the other side of the street near one of the derelict buildings,

"Hey, you wanna buy some dope?"

We thought, what kind of place is this where you scream at the top of your lungs that you have drugs to sell — to strangers on the street?

At this point, an old Mexican man wandered up to us on the sidewalk. He was staggering wildly, clutching a bottle of wine. He began to engage us in conversation, for the most part drunk and disconnected chatter. He told us his name was "Silver" and we gave him our names as well. We told him we were from Iowa and had hitchhiked to LA to visit our girlfriends. The wine had him in an amicable mood and he made the comment, if we needed anything, he would help. We thanked him and lost no time cramming into the phone booth and placed the call we had traveled so far to make. Carrie answered — sort of. It didn't sound like her at all. The voice was curt and cold.

"Carrie?"

"Yeah," she said with obvious indifference.

"It's me. We made it! We're here!"

"Yeah," she repeated.

"How do we get to your place?"

She then uttered the words that nearly made my knees buckle.

"You can't come here. My parents won't allow it!"

"WHAT?" I said in disbelief. "Where are we supposed to go?"

She matter of factly replied, "I don't know, but if you're not off the streets by 10:00 the police will take you to the LA County Jail."

Ten o'clock was less than an hour away.

One hundred percent depleted, physically and emotionally drained, we had used every drop of reserved energy and willpower we had. We were starving and had lost at least 10 pounds apiece. Stunned, in just minutes Mike and I had gone from valiant boyfriends making a victorious entry into the city, to desperados facing apprehension and lock-up in the Los Angeles County Jail! It was terrifying and as Mike was piecing together the conversation I was having on the phone with Carrie, his visage changed dramatically. He was leaving for his "safe zone." I knew, for all practical purposes, I was now on my own. Though totally bewildered at Carrie's radical shift from an obsessively loving and sweet girlfriend to this treacherous Jezebel, my immediate jeopardy demanded I shelve that concern and focus solely on survival. I peered through the telephone booth glass at "Silver" wandering in a drunken delirium across the street.

LA, Treachery and Silver

My mind raced as I reviewed my miserable choices for help and support; Carrie, who was ready to hang up on me … Mike, resting comfortably in a non-conscience state … and Silver, dangerously intoxicated! I looked ahead towards the street just in time to see a police cruiser drive by! I desperately implored Carrie, now having about the same influence (and social status) as Silver!

"Carrie, we have no money, we haven't eaten in days, and we have nowhere to go!"

"If you come by tomorrow, I'll give you guys something to eat, but you can't stay. I've got to get off the phone." She hung up.

I opened the phone booth door and said to Mike, "Come on, we've got to get something to eat."

Mike slowly turned and followed me, zombie-like, to the nearby McDonald's. I bought a plain small hamburger with our last 35 cents and tore it in half. Our "last meal"! Our stomachs barely registered the feeding. I walked over to Silver and desperately tried to engage him in some basic, coherent dialogue in hopes of finding shelter from the streets and police.

"Hey, Silver, where are you going to sleep tonight?" I asked.

"In my house, you idiot," was his response.

"Where do you live?" I continued, ignoring his rude reference to me.

"I live right there," he said, pointing to one of the nearby row houses. I had a flicker of hope as I looked towards Mike to see if he was tracking any of this. He wouldn't even make eye contact.

"We don't have any place to stay Silver," I said, hoping to strike a compassionate chord with him.

"You stay with me," he said.

I guess everything *is* relative. Before the call to Carrie, the prospect of staying with Silver would have been like cleaning public restrooms! Now it seemed like a Godsend.

Silver's demeanor, we would learn, was subject to radical shifts from moment to moment. He would alternate between brotherly love and serious confrontational aggression. Nonetheless, we were shackled to him in a desperate attempt to avoid jail.

Silver stumbled into his house (at least we prayed it was his house) with Mike and me cautiously following. It was atrocious — filthy and unkempt with a stench that strongly suggested something had died in the place — days ago! I remember seeing a partially eaten bean burrito sitting on top of the refrigerator with a layer of dust on it. We all sat down and Silver began to ceremoniously pass his bottle of wine to us. I intuitively sensed this to be some sort of bonding custom among street people and alcoholics. We had no choice: we had to accept the offer. To have declined would have surely destroyed the relationship we hoped to be forming. I shudder when I think back to drinking from the same bottle as Silver, who may have been a walking petri dish for every virus, bacteria and disease in the SW United States and Mexico! I didn't even like drinking after Mike.

We soon agreed it was time to retire and the prospect of sleep was welcomed. For only the second time in weeks Mike and I were resting in a solid, non-moving shelter with four walls and eight foot ceilings. We felt like battered sailors coming into a rough port after a long voyage in a turbulent and untrustworthy sea.

We dug out our sleeping bags — more to shield us from the filth than anything else — and situated ourselves on the living room floor. Silver's bed was a fold-out couch that appeared to have been in the bed position for years. I discreetly observed as Silver disrobed. He stripped down to his underwear revealing one of the most disgusting sights I had seen in my 17 years! His briefs were no longer brief. They hung from all sides, like Spanish moss and were of a similar dingy color and porosity. Full of holes, they begged the question, why? What purpose did this garment serve? In what appeared to be a customary prelude to his lying down, Silver carefully scratched and rubbed select areas of his body loosely covered by this vintage underwear. As I observed the ritual I resolutely vowed I would surrender to the county jail before drinking after this man again!

I noticed as we were crawling into our sleeping bags that Silver had not fully laid down. He was in a semi-reclined position and intently looking our way. Ultimately he revealed the nature of his interest and declared to Mike,

"You sleep with me!"

In his inebriated state, and with the dimmed lighting, Silver now perceived Mike to be female, due no doubt to Mike's long hair.

"No, that's ok," Mike answered quietly, as though he had been offered an hors d'oeurve.

Silver was undaunted at the rejection, "You sleep with me, I no wet the bed!"

"No," Mike said. "I'm alright down here."

Mike's voice lacked a firm tone. His resistance was polite and weak and I believe in Silver's demented state he may have viewed it as Mike playfully toying with him. That, in fact, this rather rough-looking girl with the broken front tooth was playing hard to get. The back and forth courtship went on for some time. Despite being in a drunken stupor, Silver relentlessly maintained his amorous pursuit. Eventually, he surrendered to the effect of the wine and passed out.

At last, Mike and I could have some peace, we thought, as we submitted to a deep sleep….

Less than an hour later we were abruptly awakened by Silver shouting,

"What you doing in my house? What you doing in my house?"

He was storming around the room, haphazardly searching the chairs and the floor.

"I shoot you! Where my gun? I shoot you!"

I desperately tried to talk Silver down, reminding him who we were and how he had invited us to spend the night, but to no avail. He remained in a highly agitated drunken rage as he continued to search for his firearm. I closely watched his every move, knowing if he located a gun I would be forced to make a lightning fast tackle on him. In those seconds, a couple of grim possibilities flashed through my mind. One, of course, was getting shot. Another, was the police arriving due to the disturbance. I could just see the uncompromising officers looking at me, holding Silver's gun, with Silver screaming we had broken into his house! And we thought this was going to be our refuge, our safe haven off the streets!

My dad once told me to remember, "No matter how bad things are, they can always get worse." I was finding that to be true. In the ensuing days, shoes would continue to drop — one tragedy after another — with a seemingly endless capacity for deeper despair. A harsh contrast to the anticipated joy California and the twins were promised to bring!

Finally, a combination of soft, sensible reassurance and the sedative effect of the wine again had Silver asleep on his bed. I don't believe Mike and I slept all night. Silver's capricious behavior with a tendency toward sexual deviancy or murder dispelled any notion we had of dozing. Little did we know the following day would be the beginning of a marathon that would easily exceed anything we had experienced so far — a marathon we would be forced to begin after days of no food (save 2 bites) and a 24-hour period of no sleep!

Next morning, Silver arose and greeted us,

"How you doing?"

It was as though the night before had been unremarkable. I believe it had simply been a routine night in the life of a pitiful alcoholic. Apparently, he had some recollection of who we were but I believe most of the events of the previous night were not present at all in his memory. We responded in kind and exchanged some small talk. We quickly gathered our things, bid Silver adios, and hit the streets. We hoped we'd never see Silver again.

Chapter 9
Carrie and Cassie — The Reunion

We had expected some fireworks upon our arrival in L.A. But not like this! We hadn't slept. Other than 2 bites of a very modest hamburger we hadn't eaten in 3 or 4 days. Our predicament (we thought) couldn't be worse. No food, no money, no girlfriends, no help, and very little hope! And 2,000 miles from home! With "beaucoup" troubles to choose from, the radical shift of the twins' dispositions dominated the list.

Ironically, a popular song debuted on radio stations around the country almost immediately following our trip to L.A. The striking similarities to our experience were uncanny. The song was titled "It Never Rains in Southern California", by Albert Hammond – though "The Ballad of Mike and Jake*" would have been equally appropriate! Excerpts as follows:

Seems it never rains in
Southern California,
Seems I've often heard that
Kind of talk before.
It never rains in California
But girl don't they warn ya
It pours, man it pours

Out of work, I'm out of my head
Out of respect
I'm out of bread (money)
I'm underloved, I'm underfed
I wanna go home
It never rains in California
But girl don't they warn ya
It pours, man it pours

**My nickname back then.*

Seems it never rains in
Southern California
Seems I've often heard that
Kind of talk before.
It never rains in California
But girl don't they warn ya
It pours, man it pours

Hearing the song would instantly return me to the California ordeal for decades. It still does.

Mike and I talked as we hitchhiked, or I should say walked. Hitchhiking is difficult in the city. On the open road traffic is typically more sparse and a shoulder is usually available for a vehicle to pull over on without impeding traffic. In the city, for a driver to negotiate a stop could mean getting rear-ended. Consequently, when thumbing in the city, you resign yourself to do a lot of walking. We wound up walking most of the way to Carrie and Cassie's house. That allowed us ample time to try to understand what dynamics could be involved to cause this tragic turn in the girls' attitudes.

First, it seemed appropriate to reflect on the previous night (or nightmare). It certainly hadn't been dull. As our excursion thus far had been almost exclusively one disaster after another, I felt compelled to infuse a little humor.

"So, Mike, what about the spat last night? Did you and Silver ever make up?"

"I can't believe you just acted like you were asleep," Mike responded angrily.

"What was I supposed to do?" I said. "Jump up and defend your honor, like you were my girlfriend?"

"Well," Mike said, "you didn't have to act like you were asleep!"

Mike didn't get it — that it likely wouldn't have dissuaded Silver had I intervened. The man was delirious. He may have thought he had two women there if I joined the party!

"Besides," I continued, "I felt kind of sorry for old Silver."

"What?" Mike said incredulously. "He was a pervert!"

"Well," I explained, "anyone desperate enough to go after a girl as ugly as you is a pitiful man."

"Yeah," Mike countered, "I think you should move in and be Silver's roommate. *You* could cuddle up with him!"

Mike was not a sissy. However, his expecting to be rescued by me in stressful situations was evidence of his mother's over-doting in his rearing. Another example was Mike's escapes to his "safe zone" during times of crises. I believe there was a little boy inside him yelling, "Mom, help!" He had simply never developed defense mechanisms to deal with challenging events.

The topic turned to the 800 lb. twin gorillas that were hitchhiking with us. We had to try to get some idea of what had happened. We desperately needed to prepare a strategy to resolve this calamity. Our lives depended on it. It seemed hopeless, though. Carrie had been so resolute, so cold, as to send the message there was no compromise in the matter. And, it couldn't have been just the parents disagreeing with our visit. Carrie's malicious demeanor seemed to be clear evidence of that — very personal. She expressed disdain, even hostility toward us.

When we last saw the girls, all four of us were in "Kodiak Bear Love"! Carrie, I believed, would have taken a bullet for me — and of course Mike and I had just demonstrated our love for the girls by taking numerous bullets clear across the United States. Actually, more like assault weapon fire! We ultimately came to a consensus. One, we had no idea why the girls were doing this or what was going through their minds. And two, we would discover the problem and fix it. We had to! We began to have a little hope — maybe due to lack of sleep — until we turned the corner and the twins' home came clearly into view. The sight was devastating. They say every picture tells a story. This picture told two stories. First, it answered all the questions of this mystery. Secondly, it destroyed all hope of reconciliation.

The first time we laid eyes on Carrie and Cassie they were frolicking in the water at Lewis' Lake. Today we saw them frolicking again on their front porch — with what appeared to be their hometown lovers! Two young Mexican men, probably in their early 20's, sat on the porch, like kings, with the girls giggling as they catered to them! They seemed to enjoy our humiliation as Mike and I came into view. The presentation appeared scripted or at least dramatized and exaggerated. Had our hunger not been such a dire matter we would have turned and left, but to where? We walked towards the house. Words can't adequately convey the devastation we felt. I expected Mike to collapse. How do you mistake you and your girlfriend being in love? Mike and I would have (and indeed) risked life and limb for these girls. How could this have been so one sided? Had we simply been a summertime fling while the girls were on vacation? How could that be? What about the excitement and love we felt on the beach? The kisses on those nights we would sneak away to East Moline? Were they counterfeit? They sure didn't feel like it. And the tears? *All* those tears? Mere days ago I had everything in life I could ever want. To have a girl as sweet and beautiful as Carrie whisper in my ear, "I love you…!" Now I couldn't believe the scene in front of me!

Carrie came out to us in the yard, not to greet us but rather to let us know to remain by the curb. Clearly, talk of our past or future relationship was no longer relevant.

Carrie and Cassie – The Reunion

We were young but capable of profoundly deep emotions. In Carrie's case, malevolency, in mine, heartbreak. I know Mike was devastated too. Cassie? She receded into the shadows and her disposition towards these developments would remain forever unknown. I sensed Carrie had devised and quarterbacked the treachery. She was the dominant of the twins and immediately took control of the execution of events when Mike and I reached their home.

I made no mention of our doomed relationship but rather addressed the more pressing matters. Food and shelter. Carrie immediately declared we couldn't stay there. The comment was preemptive as I hadn't repeated the request. She was well-prepared to execute an entirely choreographed and elaborate conspiracy to effectively (and nearly literally), "kick us to the curb," but also do so in a fashion that would take us far from her home. She was particularly careful to demonstrate the highest degree of hostility so as to dissuade us from regarding her or her home as a refuge. In retrospect, regardless of the reason for her loss of affection for me (If that ever truly existed), I believe her foremost objective was to never let her parents know what she had done to Mike and me. To have lured us, walking, through a 2,000 mile gauntlet for an incredible rendezvous in the exotic place we had dreamed of — and then ruthlessly offer the county jail as an alternative! Though I will never know with certainty, my hunch is Carrie told her parents Mike and I decided not to make the journey to California, once her and Cassie made the decision to reunite with their local boyfriends. Their villainy would face exposure should their parents ever lay eyes on Mike and me in town, or worse yet talk with us! Consequences for the girls would likely be dire. Carrie wanted us gone — fast!

Carrie told me, stoically, that one of her girlfriends was in route to her house. This girl, "Cindy", resided with friends in a cabin out on Seal Beach. She might be able to arrange for us to stay there.

"She'll be here anytime," Carrie said as she turned and walked back to the porch.

"Carrie, you said you'd give us some food," I called to her.

"Oh, yeah," she said in a disgusted tone. "I'll be right back."

She returned in less than five minutes with 2 plates. On each plate were 2 half-fried eggs with the whites still semi-translucent.

"Carrie, do you have any toast?" I pleaded, like an inmate to the jailer.

She looked angry, went back to the house and returned with 1 piece of bread, not toast, for each of us. At this point I'm thinking, how much worse could the county jail be?

As we were eating this "great food" Carrie had promised, I thought for a moment about how little it mattered now how cool she looked in a swimsuit. Additionally, if this was retribution for what we had done to the Alaska-bound men or the innocent boys in Cheyenne, it was being repaid ten-fold.

The meal was nearly a nothing event and soon, as precision-planned, Cindy arrived. She played her part very well. Kind, smiling, and hope-inspiring. She said she believed the people she stayed with on the beach would accommodate us. Cindy, we would later discover, was the "ice-lady" — the "executioner". She instructed us to head to the beach but did not give us the beach house address. Rather, she told us to wait near a particular concession stand. She also informed us she could not get there until 11:00 p.m.

Mike and I departed for Seal Beach. We had hopes of a change of luck — anemic ones at best. But maybe these people at the beach house would be kind. To be staying right on the water! We could enjoy the ocean for a few days, waiting for money from mom, then head back home. Might be okay. Neither of us really believed that.

The trip across LA was only approximately 20 miles, but it would seem like crossing Asia. Not only were the freeways terrifying, fast, confusing, and complex, our greatest obstacle would be the unreliability of the people who gave us rides. Each driver was an "expert" on the area and would instruct us precisely which route to follow — or face disaster! Yet the very next driver would soundly disqualify and ridicule the previous driver's advice!

"Oh, no, that makes no sense at all! I don't know why anyone would ever tell you that! Here's what you need to do…"

Seal Beach lay due south. However, during the course of that dreadful day we zig-zagged, headed straight east for miles, then traveled north almost out of LA doing numerous "U"- turns in the process. I really didn't know if all the misinformation was intentional or not — or if we had descended into some kind of hellish dimension where we would eternally traverse the freeways of Los Angeles in a starving and sleep-deprived mode! Our city map was well-worn from scribblings and countless foldings and unfoldings. It looked as though it had gone through a washing machine. I saved it for a long time as a memento, until the gloom of reviewing it overwhelmed me.

At long last we made it to Seal Beach. It had been a nearly unbearable day and darkness had fully settled. We were physically exhausted and nearly devoid of any hope for the future. We found the designated benches by the concession stand around 10:00 p.m. The stand was closed and though we knew the water was roughly 100 yards away, we could not visualize it because of the dunes and darkness. But we could hear it and our spirits revived! Carrie and Cassie had turned out to be unfaithful wenches (or witches) but not our truer love. She had waited patiently, and we could hear her calling to us, lovingly — with soft, soothing sounds. Weeks of torment and pain were instantly rescinded.

"Oh, wow," I whispered to Mike for fear of someone hearing me (though the beach was obviously deserted). "Do you think that's the ocean we're hearing?"

"Got to be," was Mike's equally naive reply.

"Let's go see," I suggested, momentarily ignoring our disaster.

"Better not," Mike cautioned. "If we miss Cindy, we are in trouble. She's our last hope."

We continued listening to the mesmerizing waves until Cindy literally stepped out of the darkness like a ghost!

"How are you guys doing?"

"Oh, we're okay," I said, a little startled. "What did you find out?"

"I haven't asked the guys at the cabin yet. I wanted to make sure you made it."

She said she'd go check with them and be right back. About 15 minutes later Cindy returned, and I immediately noticed her smile was missing. She had the same cold look that Carrie had displayed earlier in the day. Her attitude had also changed dramatically. This was the end-point of the evil collusion the girls had planned so well.

"They're not going to let you stay," Cindy proclaimed in a cold, calm, and firm tone.

"Oh, really," I pleaded. "We won't take up much space, the floor is fine, and we won't eat anyth——"

"No," Cindy interrupted, "you can't stay there."

Talk about deja-vu. It had been almost exactly 24 hours since Carrie had pronounced the same sentence on us but this time the dialogue didn't even get to the point of "Where are we supposed to go?" Cindy beat me to it, and offered the merciless warning, "If the beach police find you sleeping in the dunes they will take you to jail." Oh my gosh, I thought, did these girls come straight from hell? With breathtaking apathy, Cindy had delivered the "kill shot"!

Mike reacted predictably. One glance revealed he had left his body with me, warm but unresponsive, and had mentally taken up residence elsewhere — maybe the ocean.

Without even a good-bye, Cindy turned and disappeared into the darkness — like a hangman! It was eerie! Did Cindy even live on Seal Beach? She may have lived 3 blocks from the twins and had simply driven to the beach for the charade. Carrie knew how badly Mike and I longed to see the ocean —— an easy place to mislead us to — and far from the twins home. The event, scheduled late into the night, may have provided cover so Mike and I would not see her enter a car instead of a beach house. In any event, the twin's cold-hearted deception was incredible. Our health or safety was of no concern to them — at all. They could have at least lured us eastward, back towards the Midwest. Instead, they misguided us to the furthest point west in the country!

We sat there, devastated. Like two innocent defendants who had just been wrongly convicted and sentenced! We were young and resilient but everything has its limits. Mike's inert state left me trying to strategize alone. Sometimes he would answer me, sometimes not. When he did, his input was so altered by his mental state as to be without substance. Before we left on this fateful journey I had given my mother a final telephone call to say good bye. Being the typical worrying mother, she offered me some information. Information that might save us should we find ourselves in peril in California. She gave me the name of her sister who she hadn't seen or talked to in years, along with her address. Her name was Helen and Mom said she was a wonderful woman who lived in San Diego, just 120 miles south of LA. I took out my billfold and desperately searched for the scrap of paper I was sure I'd never need. I tried to revive Mike with this hopeful prospect but it was like talking to a stump.

We were entering our second day without sleep and our bodies were in dire need of food, particularly given the rigorous stresses of the summer heat and constant hiking in the sun. It had been days since we had eaten a meal. We also had only occasional access to water. At this point I was confident we had exceeded the hardships of Marine boot camp training and were more in the Special Forces torture arena. The type that leaves only a couple of the entire group standing.

I finally got Mike to agree to get up and push on, south towards San Diego. We had lingered a long time on the bench, lost in despair, and it was now well past midnight — a terrible time to hitchhike!

As we turned to leave I looked back towards the ocean — 2000 hard miles and not even a glimpse … the second heartbreak that day.*

**30 years would pass before I finally got to "see, touch, smell, and swim" in the Pacific Ocean!*

Chapter 10
Dark Abyss / Blazing Sun

We made our way out to I-5 and turned south toward San Diego. The night was pitch black, as were our spirits. Mike lay on the ground, several feet off the shoulder of the road, a common practice for him, as I hitchhiked. I was in a hyper-awake state, partially due to biological dysregulation and also the numerous emotions surrounding and taunting me. Missing the Midwest, my mom, and the comforts and stability of home. Food was a constant thought. Even sleep was now an elusive luxury. Uncertainties and fears tormented me. *How will we get home? What part of San Diego did Helen live in? Mom hadn't talked to her in years. Was she still alive? I'm thirsty. When will I get a chance to get some water? There are no gas stations in sight...*

I did acknowledge one paradoxically positive thing. Carrie had made the break clean. This was not death by a thousand small cuts. It was one quick and massive mortal wound! We were spared the typical struggles and heartache of a faltering relationship. I don't believe Mike and I ever discussed the twins again. But I would never forget! Their deception and cut-throat treatment of us had been so severe, so malevolent, so undeserved that it immediately and forever removed any trace of affection we had for them. I could never have imagined entirely losing my love for Carrie in a 24 hour period — but it was gone! The Kodiak Bear collapsed!

The loneliness out there on the road that night was incredible. The night was so dark I could barely make out Mike, just several feet from me. Approaching drivers were alarmed when only at the last minute they spotted me in their headlights. Of course when drivers could only see me when they were on top of me there was little inclination to stop. It was more like, "Whoa, what was that?" They would swerve, wildly, and drive on. I probably resembled a frightened animal — exactly what I felt like. I wanted to surrender to the despair, like Mike, and lay down beside him — but alas, I was the captain. If we both capitulated we were really in trouble. Who would save us then?

Rides were hard to come by that night. Mutual fearfulness, I believe, prevailed. Granted, hitchhiking was commonplace during this era, however, why on earth would two young men be thumbing rides in the dead of night or the wee hours of the morning? On the run? High on drugs? We had formerly used a nighttime hitchhiking strategy (with little success) but we didn't go past 10 or 11 p.m. This time was different. We had no choice. We desperately needed help.

Understandably, we had cause for concerns of our own. Why would a *driver* be on the road at these odd hours? Granted, there could be totally benign reasons. People on the last leg of a long trip. Those who worked unusual shifts, etc. But there were also criminals out there, mental degenerates, sexual predators, and murderers — many strange people who would prefer the cover of darkness. Mike and I had received rides from some scary people. It's true we had the advantage of being a pair but a handgun could quickly eliminate that leverage. All our fears that night (actually my fears as Mike slumbered) were heightened, I believe, by several things. It being the eerie middle of the night, the absolute blackness of that night, and the marked effects of our food and sleep deprivation. One thing I knew for sure — we weren't in Iowa anymore!

Rides came infrequently and for surprisingly short distances. Still, I was grateful, not only to get closer to what hopefully would be our long-sought sanctuary but also because it forced Mike to wake up and talk to me. His contribution was minimal and rather muted yet still it provided a sense of companionship.

We hitchhiked through the night and eventually caught a ride with a man who would take us nearly all the way to San Diego. He told us he was a former military man and had a soft spot for hitchhikers as he had done some of that during his time in the army while on leave (a common practice for service members then). He asked if we were military, which I found a little incredible. Indeed we had luggage, were hitchhiking and were approximately military age, but our hair, especially Mike's, I thought should have easily disqualified us. We obviously fit the hippie profile far more than the clean-cut, well-dressed serviceman. He dropped us off a few miles outside San Diego and bid us farewell.

There was always a sort of sadness that came with leaving our host ride. I'm not sure why. We had typically only known them a relatively short period of time and in a non-intimate way. I guess there was security in the car, albeit temporary, and the return to the road brought back the almost certain threat of heat, sun, rain, police, and a host of the unknown.

We were still some distance outside the city when the powerful southern California sun began to rise. It was warm and welcomed and furthermore I knew it would spell an end to Mike's somnolent retreats.

"Hey Mike, you know what we need to be doing?"

"Yeah," Mike quipped. "We need to be back home in bed."

"No, seriously Mike, we need to be spare-changing these people we get rides with. Not during the ride — they might not like it and drop us off — but when we're getting out. What do you say?"

"Good idea," Mike agreed. "I'm starving!"

"Why don't you get into that same pitiful mode that got you that big spaghetti dinner," I suggested.

"I don't have to 'get into that mode', I'm already there," Mike declared.

It was true. We couldn't have been more qualified. I don't know how it had escaped us. We had spare-changed many times on a full stomach. Now, when we were truly starving, it hadn't even occurred to us!

Our next ride was with an obviously wealthy man. He drove a luxury car and wore a suit and expensive jewelry. I thought this scenario could definitely yield spaghetti meals. He would take us the few miles to San Diego but informed us National City, where Helen lived, was actually south of San Diego. Bummer! We would be forced to walk miles in the city! The driver pulled over and we prepared to unload. Now was our chance for food money…

"Do you have any spare-change?" I asked, adding, "We haven't eaten in several days."

His demeanor seemed to change, as though he had given us a ride and now, like ingrates, we were trying to exploit him for drug money with a bogus story of not haven eaten for days! He stated he didn't have much money, reluctantly reached into his pocket, withdrew 2 quarters and handed them to us. We thanked him and exited the car.

We wasted no time in crossing the street to the gas station and, (regressively?), proceeded directly to the candy shelves. Actually, we knew we lacked enough money for bread and cold-cuts or really any type of food that would resemble a meal. I remember scanning the shelves for the biggest candy bar I could find. (Candy bars sold for 25 cents then.) "Big Boy" (I'll call it) stood out prominently. It was a decisively low-end ingredient type of taffy bar. Quantity, not quality — exactly what I wanted! I don't remember what Mike bought, other than it was also candy. We sat outside the store and enjoyed the food (if that's an appropriate term). For me it was sort of an attraction/repulsion experience. Loving the fact I was placing *anything* technically edible in my stomach, yet finding the taste and texture seriously lacking. Loving the old familiar feeling of actually exercising my teeth and salivary glands, yet wearing out my tongue dislodging the goo from every crevice of my mouth. The consistency was similar to what I imagined roofing tar would be. That is, once

I got it worked up. I'm confident if I would have had any leaks in my mouth "Big Boy" would have fixed them! The "meal" wasn't what we'd hoped for but at least we had taken on some calories.

The sun, no longer our friend, had totally transformed into a cruel taskmaster, following close on our heels — punishing us with unrelenting and unbearable heat! There was no place to hide! We had to struggle on towards our last hope for help… Helen's house!

Neither Mike nor I had experienced a privileged upbringing. The rusty, junked VW van sitting prominently in Mike's front yard likely confirmed that. We were from poor working class families and had seen the associated hardships. But nothing like this. It reminded me of the infamous "death marches" I'd seen in war movies when prisoners were forced to walk long distances under the cruelest conditions — thirsty, starving and wounded. Granted, this was not as bad, but it was tough.*

The sun was high in the sky when we finally arrived at 1339 West Third Street in National City. We stood for a moment, in awe, staring at the modest bungalow as though we had reached Oz. Pretty flowers adorned the front porch border and comforted me — consistent with what a kind old aunt might do, I hoped. Our hesitancy seemed queer but we were both feeling it. Sort of like a long-time prisoner being released from the penitentiary and, at the last moment, being fearful of the freedom.

"Come on man!" I called to Mike as I walked up the few steps to the front door. Mike followed in his usual careful fashion. I knocked and a woman in her late 20's answered the door. She appeared pleasant and wore a smile. "Hello," she said. At the same time I heard an infant's voice babbling from inside the home. I felt dispirited as I read the entire scenario in literally a few seconds. This picture was

**By no means do I want to suggest our hardships approached the horrific suffering and sacrifices incurred by tens of thousands of our brave young men in the Vietnam War.*

not fitting the profile I had expected and hoped for. The woman had answered the door in a polite but authoritative manner not consistent with that of a guest but rather the primary owner or occupant. And the baby? This did not look good. To me it was obvious. The woman was a young housewife home with her baby while her husband was off at work. No "kind old aunts" here.

"Hi," I said in the most pleasant voice I could find. "We are from the Midwest; actually Iowa, and we hitchhiked out here to California to visit some friends. My mother told me her sister lived at this address and we came down from LA to visit. Does Helen Nolan live here?"

"No," the lady answered, "there is no Helen that lives here."

For a second I felt woozy. I didn't dare look around to see the effect on Mike.

"Oh really?" I asked, as I tried to hide my dejection, as well as days of fatigue and hunger.

"No," she said with an authentic sound of sympathy, looking straight through my façade, like only a woman can do.

"Have you lived here long?" I asked, hoping Helen may have just recently moved and left a forwarding address.

"We've been here three years," she replied.

Desperately, I continued, "Do you know anything of a woman named Helen Nolan who *used* to live here?"

"No," she said, her voice softening to almost a whisper, "I've never heard of her. Sorry."

I knew to continue the questioning would be in vain. "Well, thanks anyway," I said.

"Oh," she replied, "that's okay. I hope you find your aunt."

Mike and I descended the steps and stood on the sidewalk out front. We were two lost pups. I suspected the lady was likely observing us from the house. It was mid-afternoon and the sun was in full fury. The sweat poured from our bodies. Why our kidneys didn't shut down is a mystery. We would go the longest times without water in the searing heat. When we did quench our thirst, it was from a filthy gas station bathroom's sink faucet! Time after time! That alone should have killed us.

"What are we going to do?" I wondered aloud. My words were rhetorical as I typically could not turn to Mike for strength or guidance in times of crisis.

"I don't know," Mike answered.

At least he was talking.

"I know what I'm going to do," I said.

"What?" he asked.

"I'm going to go knock on that lady's door and ask if we can sleep in her backyard for a couple of hours."

"You can't do that," Mike said firmly.

"Mike, I'll tell her our story, how down and out we are. How we ran out of money and food. She's a nice lady. She'll understand."

"That would be the dumbest thing we've ever done," Mike argued.

"No, Mike, it's not! I haven't been to sleep in 2 ½ days! I can't just turn around and start walking again — clear across the city! I've got to have some sleep!"

The argument continued, though I don't know where we found the strength. Mike and I rarely disagreed. I really couldn't understand why he wanted to go back to LA so badly. There was nothing there for us.

I calmly walked up to the woman's door and knocked. She answered with the same kind demeanor.

"Um, I'm sorry to bother you again but me and my friend were sort of betrayed by the people we came to LA to visit. We ran out of money and food and we haven't slept in over 2 days. Would you mind if we caught a couple hours sleep in your backyard?"

"No," she said, "I wouldn't mind. Just go around the side and let yourself in the gate." The lady was an angel.

Mike followed me around the house, bitterly disputing the decision the entire way — muttering disapproval and disgust like some old senile man in an institution. I was thinking he and Silver could have really communicated at this point.

My dad's words came back to me. "No matter how bad things are, remember, they can always get worse." Remarkably, my brother's boot camp sorrows occurred just a couple miles away at the marine base! A Bermuda Triangle for our family?

We got to the backyard where I calmly ignored Mike's continued objections and collapsed on the grass. I remember thinking, I usually can't get Mike to talk — now I can't get him to stop! His combativeness was a stark deviation from his normal disposition. I think the trauma of the last few days was doing strange things to him. His reasoning was illogical. Why the desperation to get back to LA?

"I can't believe we're doing this," he began again. "It's so stupid to ask someone we don't even know to sleep in their yard. This is the dumbest thing we've ever done!"

"I don't know, Mike, we've done some pretty dumb things." My attempt at mitigating the tension with a joke was not successful. It simply fueled Mike's anger.

"Okay," he declared in a very commanding voice, "you stay here and sleep, I'm going to LA. I'll see you back there!" As though we had a familiar part of town where we would be bound to bump into each other!

I couldn't take any more. I hadn't been able to cat nap all night like Mike. I had no strength to continue the fight. "Okay," I said calmly, signaling my resolve. The last thing I remember before losing consciousness was looking over and seeing Mike rolling out his sleeping bag and shaking his head. He was still talking to himself, "…so stupid…I can't believe we're doing this … sleep in some stranger's yard …"

Chapter 11
Silver Revisited

It was late afternoon when the sun resumed his command. We were soaked in sweat. Our sleeping bags hadn't helped. Besides providing a cushion they had also held the heat that poured from our bodies. It was like sleeping in a sauna and probably as dangerous. The sleep, though not ideal, did help somewhat. As I mention again (and again) going days without food is difficult. To do it while physically pushing hard in the summer sun with minimal water is another animal altogether. Mike and I awoke to yet another day in our endless nightmare!

We packed up our stuff and began the marathon back across San Diego. It was dusk by the time we made it through the city to the open road heading north. I really didn't know what was pulling us back to LA, but the lure was strong. It certainly wasn't fond memories or a shelter from the storm. In fact, LA's strict curfew, our fear of that big city jail, and our past experiences there should have made it our last choice. Despite those considerations and with little discussion (or thought), we decided to make Silver's place our destination. Indeed, he had wanted to molest Mike and later threatened to kill us — which you would think would give him a "poor host" rating — but we were two desperate hombres! We had to have a place off the streets, an address to receive money from home. Maybe Silver's tirade had been a stark aberration. He had been much kinder the following morning…

We were on the watch for a rest area. We badly needed water and sleep. Food was not an option. Midway to LA we asked our ride if he would drop us off at an approaching rest area. This marked the first time we had ended a ride short of its maximum potential. The driver kindly accommodated and we wasted no time in filling up on water. We then scoped out the area, looking for a secluded spot to bed down, one obscure from headlights should a highway patrolman scan the grounds on drives through. We found a good location and spread out our sleeping bags. Mike was asleep almost instantly, while I lay there looking at the stars.

I thought about several things, foremostly food. The hunger pangs do subside somewhat after a certain point but are replaced by a more intense urgency to eat — or die! I believe it happens when your body reacts to using strictly fat or muscle for fuel. I don't think we were burning muscle yet, though our fat reserves were definitely being depleted. We were indeed at "fighting weight". Prominent abdominal muscles belied our true condition. Our BMI would have been an envy to many, including Mike's mom. Might have bolstered her faith in the diet soup!

To lie in the thick grass in the cool of the summer night was heavenly. The breeze softly caressed my face as my spirit drank in the healing comfort of this temporary oasis. This night's sleep would be precious. I realized the demands of our constant battles had precluded us from dwelling much on homesickness. I guess it would take quite the optimist, however, to be excited about that. I watched the stars with the occasional jet traffic between San Diego and LA. I had only dreamed of being in such a famous place so far from Iowa but it had held nothing but sorrow and distress. And Carrie? I would trade everything in California to be back at Lewis' Lake — on the blanket with Kim. (Okay, Mike, too!)

We were awakened by merry little travelers laughing and chattering, piling out of their parents' cars, heading for the restrooms and water fountains. Mike and I rolled up our bags and did likewise before resuming our precarious journey. Looking back, I'm amazed at how incidental bathroom visits were for Mike and me — how long we would go without distress. It's a whole different scenario for older adults, women, and little children. On airplane flights, the plane barely gets off the ground and we have a line forming in the aisle.

Not a teenage boy in the bunch! Same thing in the theater. Previews of upcoming movies haven't even finished and we see people sheepishly passing the screen, yes, already in dire need of a bathroom visit! Mike and I could have been out on the open road for half a day and catch a ride. If the guy was going 200 miles, we wouldn't even have considered asking him to make a pit stop. I'm guessing the average 17 year old male can go 4 days without using the bathroom! On the other hand, our food and fluid intake was scant at best. If frequent trips to the bathroom are a bother, our experience proved that fasting for days with long periods of no water in the summer sun will pretty much stop the problem!

Even though our predicament was reaching a truly critical level we could think of no source of help. As I mentioned, I was a minor. We couldn't simply go to a social service agency and seek assistance, as they would immediately alert the police, who would take me into custody until picked up by a legal guardian. The second problem we feared was LA's strictly-enforced curfew. Again, we couldn't resume the arduous journey back home without money for food and we needed an address to receive money. Silver, we felt, was our only option.

While the entire trip had been very difficult, our disposition was now quite different than before the girls' treachery. Prior to being forsaken, we had a certain destination — a fantastic asylum, replete with food and beautiful hostesses. Now, the disdain and intolerance for hippies that prevailed seemed much more threatening as we had no safety net — at all. We had lost everything! Silver, nasty underwear, alcoholism, and all, was far more protected and stable than we were! That was our grim reality. In the past when a gas station attendant would see Mike and me approaching the restrooms at his facility and quickly intercept and send us on down the road, we could accept the abasement, knowing Carrie and Cassie awaited with excellent accommodations. Now, however, we felt like hated societal outcasts. When expelled from a gas station restroom, we felt our next stop might be jail! We were totally devoid of any shelter. No one was waiting for us. No fair haven was in sight.

The trip back to LA was quick. One ride took us all the way to the city limits and the next one took us to within blocks of Silver's house.

As we approached the home we saw a somewhat welcoming sight, Silver sitting out on his porch with what obviously was his ever-present companion — a bottle of wine. It was not yet noon and Silver displayed signs of being far more lucid than the night we met.

"Hey, man, how you guys doing?" Silver's greeting was encouraging.

"Good, Silver, how about you?" I replied.

"I'm okay," he said and invited us in.

Thankfully, he did not offer to share his bottle. We talked for a while and I divulged to him how badly things had been going for us. He appeared to be sincerely sympathetic. Sadly, it seemed, the heavy drinking had been responsible for the erratic and hostile behavior we experienced at our first encounter. I related how the girls had deceived and double-crossed us and now we had no place to go. He readily offered his place as a refuge but quickly added he was sorry he had no food to give us. Apparently, Silver's limited funds went primarily for the wine. He did give some advice, however, that in time would prove valuable.

"Have you heard of the Holy Cross Mission*?" Silver asked. "It's not far from here, down on San Gabriel Boulevard. They have food there. They give you food."

Mike and I had seen homeless men hang out at a mission back in Davenport, Iowa, so we had a vague idea of what a "mission" was.

** "Holy Cross Mission" is generic as the actual name escapes me. The location as being on San Gabriel Boulevard, I believe, is accurate.*

"They let you sleep there, too," Silver added. Maybe our luck was changing. It sounded a little scary but Silver could be scary too, when fully loaded.

"Hey, man," Silver said, "I got to go do some business with a friend. You guys stay here if you want. I be back by dark."

Silver said goodbye, leaving me and Mike in his filthy home. We wondered just what kind of "business" Silver would be engaged in. We decided to forget it. We had enough worries. Being alone in the house gave us a sense of security, freedom and privacy that we hadn't felt in some time. Life in public was getting hard to bear. Watching, worrying, and being watched. There was never any peace. This free-spirited hippie pilgrimage was not what it was advertised to be. I could have given it up and never looked back. The time alone at Silver's also gave us the liberty to fully appreciate the atrocious conditions of the home. That provided a strong incentive to alternatively consider the mission. Of course we hadn't seen the mission yet, but looking at Silver's place in the full daylight was frightening. We were certainly not lounging around in the easy chairs.

Our hunger was reviving and even the squalid conditions of the home did not preclude us from scouring the cupboards and refrigerator. As we advanced, or I should say declined into the realm of street people, it was clear to us we were changing. Our standards were being further compromised. Not with malice or evil intent. We were simply evolving to survive, as we had in Wyoming. It occurred to me that the homeless, who sometimes seem so rogue, may simply be doing likewise. Pilfering someone's home under normal circumstances, of course, is reprehensible. However, Mike and I searched Silver's place without a twinge of guilt. We felt we had no choice. It was "life in the jungle".

Silver had been truthful. The cupboards were bare and the refrigerator held only a half dozen eggs. Mike and I had never cooked — anything. Not even an egg! The prospect of cooking struck fear in us. Sandwiches were a different matter. We were accomplished in the sandwich arena, confident and secure in the company of mayonnaise, thick-sliced bologna and Wonderbread.

"Cook us those eggs!", Mike ordered me. It was a given — I was inherently and always in the lead position. Particularly with any threat or risk it was understood I would be the vanguard. "Okay," I thought, "How hard can this be?" I dismissed the prospect of frying the eggs as likely being too complicated. Boiling the eggs seemed less risky. Step one, I got a sauce pan. Step two, I filled it with water. Step three, I brought it to a raging boil. Step four, I carefully inserted two eggs. To our surprise and dismay both eggs cracked and spilled their contents into the boiling water, resembling something someone had regurgitated.

"What the heck happened?" Mike demanded.

"I don't know," I said in my defense. "I put the eggs in real easy. Maybe they're bad eggs."

"No," Mike argued, "They're fine, they look good. You did something wrong!"

"Okay, Mike, I'll try it again."

Mike and I were totally unaware that a refrigerated egg will reliably crack if placed directly into hard boiling water. I repeated the exact same process until we had destroyed all six eggs, the only food in the house! We discussed the sad dilemma at length and finally reached a consensus. I had diligently followed 4 basic and perfectly logical steps. These *were* bad eggs!

Looking back, it may have been a blessing. The eggs might have been 2 years old!

Trying to appear casual, I approached the refrigerator and eyed the aged burrito still conspicuously resting there, clothed in an ever increasing layer of dust. To a well-fed person the desperate act I was considering would have been insane. To a young man who hadn't eaten in a week, it looked very much like supper.

I carefully observed the burrito. Granted, the distinctive bite marks were discouraging, but what I was really looking for was any sign of insect or parasite activity. I gently lifted the top of the flour tortilla. Nothing moved. An encouraging sign. At this point, Mike, who had been continuing a relentless and thorough search for anything edible in the kitchen, glanced over and took note of my descent into this subhuman endeavor. He immediately recognized my intention.

"No way, man," he yelled, "you can't do that!" His eyes were huge, as though he was witnessing a murder.

I ignored his comments, like a hungry lion stalking a wildebeest calf that had strayed from the herd. I took out a plate from the cupboard and a sharp knife. I rewashed both of them in the sink which was probably yet another sign of my mental decline. I laid the burrito gently on the plate and with my shirt tail cleared as much of the dust as possible with the care and precision of a doctor preparing his patient for surgery. Mike had been intently observing my actions and reversed his position entirely.

"Give me some of that!" he screamed. (Our lability was a little scary during this period.)

I utilized the knife with skill, ensuring I would definitively remove all teeth marks and associated lip/slobber borders while preserving as much of the uncontaminated burrito as possible. I tried to dispel recurring flashbacks of Silver standing bedside doing his scratching and rubbing routine. All the while Mike was distracting me with a feeding frenzy type of hyper-activity.

"Come on man!" he yelled. "Come on, cut the thing!"

Jacob Sparks

At last the procedure was complete and I threw the waste portion into the garbage. With that gone, the liberated burrito had a much more attractive, possibly even fresh look. Ever so carefully, I divided the burrito in half. Despite our powerful hunger, Mike and I realized this could seriously impact our health. We did not linger with the process. A bite, 2 chews and swallow. Another bite, 2 chews and swallow. As though the process of swallowing the thing in wholesale chunks might prevent gastroenteritis or death!

Following our "meal" Mike and I sat and discussed our two grim options. Face the filth and dangers of staying at Silver's or face the fears and uncertainties of going to the mission. As we talked we again considered the disheveled and malodorous condition of Silver's house. The thoughts of lying on that dirty floor and what Silver might do in the night was too much! His behavior was so unpredictable and potentially dangerous. What condition would he arrive home in later? Had he found his gun?

For the first time since leaving home, we had options for lodging. We gathered our things and headed towards San Gabriel Boulevard. This time we wouldn't be back.

Chapter 12
Bob and The Holy Cross Mission

San Gabriel Boulevard was bustling, both with pedestrians on the sidewalk and traffic on the street. Mike and I were acquainted with cities, or at least big towns like Davenport, Iowa, but nothing of this magnitude. We felt odd and small as we coursed through the sidewalk crowd, toting our big suitcase and backpack toward the address of the mission. Unlike being on the road with our hitchhiking ilk, we were out of place with this big-city fashionable crowd. We felt even smaller as we stood at our destination.

The front of the Holy Cross Mission building was colossal, archaic and intimidating. It obviously dated back to the early 1900's, if not the 1800's.

"Are you sure we want to do this?" Mike asked.

"Mike," I reminded him, "we don't have a choice. This is our last hope!"

Sadly, we'd seen quite a few "last hopes" come and go in the recent past. We had no idea what to expect inside. Would we check in like a motel? Would we be in separate rooms? Could we request to share a room? Would there be different meal choices? Our naivety was profound! Though our experience at the mission would prove to have redeeming value, the amenities there fell far short of the 5 star status we had experienced in the motel with the salesman.

We entered the mission in a very hesitant mode. The front door opened into a large lobby about 50 feet wide by only 15 feet deep. It had the feel of a theater lobby and we would later learn the large main room beyond held a stage. Seats no longer existed in the area before the stage though the setting suggested they once had. The lobby was uncluttered but far from pristine. The floors and walls bore signs of a lack of maintenance or thorough housecleaning.

Nothing that matched the deplorable condition of Silver's place — more similar to Mike's room back home!

We noticed a woman sitting behind a glass partition with a pass-through opening appearing very much like a ticket counter from yesteryear. She glanced over and beckoned to us. As we walked towards her I noticed Mike was lagging behind. His eyes were open wide and fixed on my back so as to avert any possible eye contact and discussion with this lady. I was fully accustomed to his "shrinking violet" behavior.

"Hi," I said. "Me and my friend are from Iowa and we hitchhiked here to LA to visit some friends, but they…" I recited the basic elements of our plight as I did almost daily now. She was polite but very matter-of-fact in her response. I'm sure she had heard and seen it all. I explained our most pressing issues were no food and no place to sleep. She stoically recited the house rules to us. To receive a meal we were required to attend the pastor's evening service at 6:00 p.m. We would be fed immediately afterward and were allowed to remain in the building until 10:00 p.m., and could then sleep on the floor in the main room. We would be awakened at 7:00 a.m. and asked to leave the premises until the 6:00 p.m. service later that day. We were informed this criterion had to be met in order to comply with local fire department regulations.

The building was modestly furnished and in a state of disrepair. I'm confident it did not meet the city's building code standards but likely was given a pass in consideration of its function to aid the homeless. I also suspect rent on the building was either waived by the owner or funded gratuitously by some benevolent soul or souls out there.

The woman's name was Joan and though not unkind, it was apparent her ongoing and unchanging routine as clerk at the mission had relegated her to monotony. I don't know if our age played a role but Joan deviated from regulations and offered us a sandwich apiece. She stipulated we would have to leave the premises though and could return later for the evening sermon.

Mike and I walked down the street a half block and discovered the pedestrian benches on which we would spend much time in the ensuing days. We carefully opened the wrappers on our food. They were a popular brand of vending machine hamburger which was typically heated in a toaster oven. No so good cold. Additionally, these donated sandwiches were significantly outdated. Apparently, they were both edible and nonpoisonous. I opened mine and, although starving, I was particularly troubled by the green and pink colors present on the inside of the bun. The green color seemed to clearly correlate with the pickle sitting directly above it, but the pink color had no identifiable source. Admittedly, I was the one who chose to eat, quite possibly, the scariest and potentially most lethal burrito in the state, but this mysterious pink color caused me notable concern. I had never encountered pink food and, frankly, it scared me. I would eat many of these burgers in the following days but never before pinching off all traces of pink on the bun. The green I left. Mike, on the other hand, ate like a hungry hobo without the slightest regard to temperature, taste, texture or color. I encouraged him to share my concern about the source and nature of the pernicious pink coloration but to no avail.

We passed many hours sitting on the benches observing and assessing passersby. I'm sure we were a far more interesting sight to behold. The pedestrians were well-dressed shoppers and business people, a stark contrast to our casual if not homeless look, babysitting our seriously out-of-style suitcase and well-worn backpack!

Six o'clock was approaching and we, unknowingly, followed the routine of numerous veteran hobos from the area and began to gravitate toward the food source — Holy Cross Mission. We arrived and joined several men who had seated themselves in folding chairs in the main room. Their boredom was readily apparent as they sat slouched with expressionless faces.

Mike and I had no experience with church matters or religion. We weren't excited about having to sit there to qualify for food. On the other hand, as we had learned, there were certainly worse things.

Bob, the mission's pastor, took his place at the head of the gathered few and introduced himself. Most of the men showed little acknowledgement Bob was even in the room, much less any semblance of respectful observance of him. Bob did, however, take particular notice of Mike and me. I wondered how this man found the perseverance to preach to a group so obviously disinterested.

I can't recall the sermon topic that evening as Mike and I were focused on the other men and the interior of the building. We weren't intentionally disrespecting Bob, just concerned about our new home and prospective roommates.

Immediately following the service the men quickly lined up in the lobby and Joan dispensed sandwiches. Two for each man and upon request a third one, designed to provide a small lunch for the following day. Of course, Mike and I requested three apiece. We had some catching up to do. Joan, knowing we were novices to the mission's routine, showed us where we would bed down. We were to simply sleep on the floor in the main room amidst numerous homeless men. She also pointed out the nearby bathroom. So much for privacy or elaborate accommodations! Certainly not what we'd hoped for, however, this had to be a *little* better than Silver's place. We might get stabbed but probably not shot! Besides, we would now phone home for money to be mailed to us. How long could a letter take to arrive? Two days, maybe three? We were confident our stay would be brief.

Immediately following the supper, Bob approached Mike and me. He began to minister to us about his past life and his personal experience with Jesus. Bob's devotion was strong and unambiguous. He was powerfully focused on us as though this was an event he had been waiting for — two young souls, destitute and providentially drawn to him, possibly as reward for his dedication in preaching to the spiritually disinclined.

Bob related to us his prior life had been that of a hobo who "rode the rails," referring to the old-time practice of hopping on freight trains to travel the country. I assumed his lifestyle was consistent with many other homeless people: drinking, stealing, malingering, fighting and surviving "in the jungle." Somewhere along his journey he had acquired a copy of the Gospel of John. He told us he read the book over and over. He had learned that God promised to bestow the gift of the Holy Spirit on any person who sincerely sought It. Bob said he continued to read the book of John and prayed for this gift of God's Spirit for three years running — and at long last, received It! This gift gave him knowledge, guidance, and comfort to direct him in all ways of his life. He said he was now "saved" and certain of his home in heaven. Bob would talk often with us in the days to come.

We discovered, because of a technical rule at the mission, we would not be able to receive mail addressed to us there. Fortunately, however, Joan advised us we could receive mail "general delivery" at the post office just down the street. Had we known that earlier we would already have been on the road! We bummed enough change on the street and made the call home. My mom and family were relieved to know we were still alive and promised to mail out $20 the following day. Help was on the way!

As I've mentioned, for the previous couple of years, maybe longer, Mike's and my obsession du jour, every jour, alternated between food and girls. Food *and* girls was a premium situation we occasionally were fortunate enough to secure. Kind of a best case scenario. Bob, however, had influenced our thoughts and conversations. Like many adolescents, we had a hunger for a deeper connection. Our interest was now drawn to what Bob had told us about Jesus and the Holy Spirit. Of course, we had heard about Jesus — Christmas and all — but Bob had revealed there was more. We were intrigued and sensed this matter was important. Maybe far more so than food or girls.

The next day Bob found us hanging out in front of the mission. He quickly seized on the opportunity and asked if we would like a Coke. We gladly accepted the offer. Bob, looking a little lost, then realized he had no money. We sensed immediately, Bob and money were strangers. Apologetically, he said, "Come on up to my room, I think I may be able to find a couple of quarters." (The price of soft drinks back then was 25cents) We followed Bob to his room where he searched the drawers, old easy chair and under the bed. He did find the 2 quarters and happily tendered them. I realized Bob was buying our time for an opportunity to share the gospel.

When my daughter Sarah was 5 years old she came to me one day with a plan she had devised to win my heart — for good. She had drawn the conclusion, that to big people, money was the most important thing. Better than birthday cake! There was always such a fuss about money. People talked about it all the time. "Do we have enough money?" "How much money does it cost?" "If we save enough money, we can go on the trip." "If I get the new job, I'll make more money." She saw adults placed an extreme value on money and seemed to have an endless obsession with it. Sarah had scoured the house for every coin she could find. A quarter here, a dime and a penny there — in a candy dish or on the kitchen counter. She carefully placed all the money in a bowl and presented the gift to me, wide-eyed, eager to see my response.

"You can have it Dad," she said proudly. "You can have *all* of it!"

Sarah was naïve to money including the pitfalls and temptations. Her only desire for money was to bring happiness to the person she gave it to. Though Bob was chronologically older, Sarah's and his heart were the same age. Bob's familiarity with money was nearly nonexistent. It was such an unusual and wonderful freedom to behold. Bob's diet was, exclusively, the ultra-plain and unappealing sandwiches. No salad, no desert, no milk and no variation. He was fine with that. His clothes were old and tattered. He lived in a tiny, dingy room on the second floor of the mission. Bob was totally free from the power of money and material things. Like Sarah, his only interest in money was giving it away.

Mysteriously, our trips to the post office yielded nothing. Several days had passed, yet no letter from home. We would periodically call my mother who assured us she had mailed the money days ago. In the meantime we continued listening to Bob, who diligently and whole-heartedly expounded to us the wonders of Christ. When he spoke of Jesus, his visage would change, markedly. His face appeared to radiate a soft glow and we could picture the scenes he described with unusual clarity, as though actually seeing them. It was truly amazing and he solidly held our attention. Bob described in great detail what Jesus would look like, glorified, in his second coming to earth. The Lord would be beautiful, with eyes of fire! Bob loved Jesus with all his heart and said he and Jesus were just like this — holding up his hand with his first two fingers crossed.

As we continued to wait for the money our spirits were faltering. It had now been nearly two weeks and we could find no explanation as to the problem. Before Mike and I discovered a refuge behind the mission, we would pass many of the daytime hours sitting on those pedestrian benches down the block. The two benches opposed each other and we would each sit on one, vis-a`-vis and talk. One day Bob found us there and with a kind smile offered us a dollar, which I suppose he had gleaned out of the mission somewhere.

"Go get yourselves an ice cream cone," he kindly suggested.

We thanked him and did just that. We returned to the bench, enjoying our treat and as I was lifting the cone toward my mouth for a lick, Mike accelerated the movement with a quick thrust of his hand under my elbow. It shoved the cone into my face, forcing the ice cream deep into my nose and eyes. He thought it was hilarious while I couldn't believe he would destroy such a rare delicacy in these hard times. Not to mention the public embarrassment as the sidewalk was always busy. I couldn't retaliate in similar fashion as Mike's cone was already gone —perhaps the impetus for the assault?

A couple of days later we were again sitting on the benches facing each other discussing our plans to get home and which route we would take. I felt an urge to sneeze and got that dopey look as I leaned forward. That calm before the storm when you are momentarily unable to function — sort of like a mini-seizure. Mike misread my pre-sneeze limbo as my wanting to whisper something to him. He responded in kind and leaned forward, placing us nearly nose to nose with that raised eyebrows, "Yeah, so what is it?" look. At that point — and with a violent jerk of my head — the powerful sneeze exploded, hitting him squarely in the face!

Even though there had been no premeditation on my part, I avoided turning my face to the side as I recalled the ice cream stunt he had previously played on me. I jumped to my feet and ran like an Olympic sprinter, knowing, there would be swift retribution. Indeed, Mike was right on my heels as I tore through the sidewalk crowd, spitting on me like a rabid animal! I ran for blocks, resembling a movie scene where the crook is haphazardly colliding with pedestrians as he zigzags to freedom. Sadly, I would not find freedom. Mike was ready to chase me into Mexico! I finally just stopped and allowed him to go berserk, until he was all out of spit. Still, he wouldn't talk to me the rest of the afternoon!

Eventually our haven down the street on the benches began to lose its appeal. As our hopelessness grew we felt more and more degraded — like outcasts on display in the town square. We asked Joan (now like a mom) if she had any ideas as to where we might go during the day when we had to vacate the mission.

"Well," she said with a hint of sympathy, "I'm not giving you guys permission to do this but some men go behind the building and sit under the trailer."

Behind the mission was an old abandoned semi-truck trailer. It had obviously been damaged beyond repair in an accident and had found its final resting place there. Mike and I enjoyed our new daytime home and embraced the privacy. It brought back memories of our hours spent in the VW van, when we would yearn for California. We now had much more somber demeanors as we again claimed a pitiful vehicle and yearned for home!

A favorite topic of discussion was food. Not the vending machine sandwiches — real food. We would take turns musing as to what we would order at the nearest restaurant when our $20 arrived. Obviously, we had learned little in regards to money management through all our hardships. Again, $20 was worth several times what it is today, still 2000 miles is a long way and restaurant food could quickly deplete our fund. Mike's final decision was cheeseburger, fries, and coke while mine was pork tenderloin sandwich, fries, and chocolate malt. Au revoir budget — Bon appetite!

Of course, reality would soon again prevail. We did, however, sense we had reached our low point, which gave us an odd sense of security. We had washed up on the shore of some island — not home, by any means, but no longer lost in the sea — not entirely safe, but certainly safer. We now had a daily routine. We knew when and where we would eat, where we would spend the day, and where we would sleep. Degraded and humiliated but stable. Kind of like a person in the intensive care unit at the hospital being upgraded and transferred to a floor. We now lived under a truck trailer in the dust with a mangy, tethered dog. We slept on a dirty floor with multiple alcoholic men. We ate outdated and discolored food. And this was the most stable and secure period of the entire excursion!

We had no idea who owned the dog. He was lean and lonely, like us. Forsaken and rejected. Sometimes we would give him half a sandwich — a generous gift. A strong bond grew. It would be hard when the money would come and we, his only friends, would also desert him.

On our last trip to the post office I pleaded with the clerk. We were on a first name basis at this point as our visits there were going on three weeks.

"I'm really sorry Jake," the postman said. "There's just nothing here for you."

"Can you please check again?" I begged. "Mom mailed the letter three weeks ago!"

He left for a lengthy period and returned, smiling ear to ear, waving an envelope above his head. He explained the dilemma. My mother had written my last name with a space between the first letter of the name and the following letters — S parks, making it appear as though the S was a middle initial and the last name was Parks. The letter had consequently been filed under the P's instead of the S's.

Our goodbyes to Bob and the dog were hard but we were overwhelmed with the prospect of heading back to the Midwest at long last.

Dorothy was right — there's no place like home!

Chapter 13
Desert Dance

Mike and I had imagined the return trip from California would be hard. Leaving our beautiful girlfriends, the beach, and all the wonderful things we had been promised. Like our Iowa goodbye to the twins — only worse. Au contraire mon frère! We were doing cartwheels. There had been periods, during the endless days and manifold hardships, when we wondered if we would ever see our native homeland again! We had been prisoners in this California house of horrors that produced a catastrophe with each new day. But now we were free, and as we promised ourselves, we scanned the horizon for the first "greasy spoon" restaurant — our particular preference! We ordered, exactly as planned, hamburger, tenderloin and fries. We hadn't eaten like this in weeks!

We had planned (reluctantly) to return to Iowa via I-80 through Nebraska but as we studied the map we saw an opportunity to bypass the NHP. We decided to consider an alternative route. One that would follow I-15 North through Las Vegas and into Utah. We could then catch I-70 east to Columbia, Missouri, and finally take the short leg north leaving me at my folk's place. Mike would continue the last 150 miles home on his own. We left the decision of I-70 vs I-80 open for the time being.

On yet the same day of our departure we decided to eat out again. We were north of San Bernardino, I believe around Victorville, and standing in a long line of hitchhikers when Mike spotted a taco stand down the road. He didn't get much resistance from me and off we went. Typically hamburgers and pizza dominated our nutritional pyramid but we certainly didn't discriminate against an occasional taco, a novelty that was just emerging on the teenage diet scene. Mothers enjoyed treating their kids and friends with this new and exciting treat — albeit the sauce, at least originally, was extremely mild. About the same Ph as milk!

The tacos at the stand were authentic and the "salsa roja" Jose advertised on the front glass with heat waves radiating upward commanded respect, even among the Latinos. The sauce they kept in the back room — I believe with the insecticides and degreasing agents!

"Give us the red sauce," I proudly boasted to Jose. He gave me that same look my brother gave me as he watched Mike and me leave for California —but complied. We gave it the old college try but it must have been a Midwestern college! We had spent $5 at the greasy spoon restaurant and now $2 more for tacos we couldn't eat, and we weren't even out of California! Now let's see — we spend one third of our return trip fund … we have traveled 83.5 miles … this seems vaguely familiar!

Our burning lips would remind us of our indiscretion as we rejoined our fellow hitchhikers out on the road. Most of them were older and wiser and sensing our obvious immaturity offered some pertinent advice on another matter.

"Don't take a ride unless they're going all the way to Barstow. Getting dropped off in the desert can be dangerous!"

As was our customary strategy, Mike and I distanced ourselves far from the others. We also composed a little jingle and dance.

"♫Now we know, not to go, unless it's clear to Barstow♪!"

Being on the return leg of our journey gave us the courage to take adversities in stride.

Indeed, our strategy proved effective and a man stopped for us, being far past the crowd — and yes he took us the 30 miles to Barstow. Our driver dropped us off at a gas station at the edge of town. We got a coke and 2 post cards and mailed them home. At this stage of my life, with fledgling frontal lobes struggling for traction, I would frequently say (or do) things that reflected a complete absence of thought, as we know it. "This is exactly what the desert looks like" is a good example, as I wrote on the post card to my mother, "Ma".

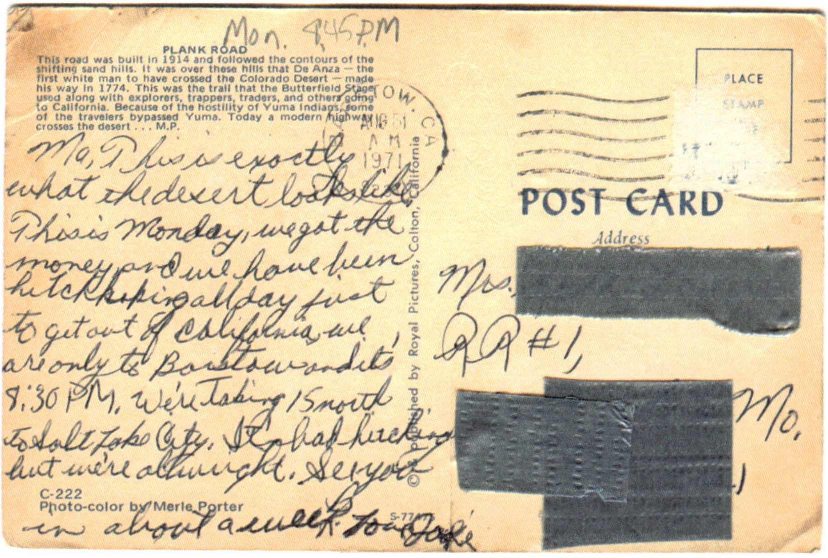

Again we found ourselves amongst a large line of hitchhikers and again they counseled us sternly — repeating what we had previously heard.

"Don't take a ride that's not going all the way across the desert!"

The warning packed even more weight as the span to cross this section of the Mohave was greater than the 30 miles from Victorville to Barstow — in excess of 100 miles!

We met two girls in this group who appeared to be in their early 20's. It seemed nearly all the hitchhikers in the country were in their early 20's, with few exceptions. We enjoyed exchanging stories. The usual, where we originated from, where we had been and our current destination. Like us, they had surmised distancing themselves from the throng would appreciably enhance their prospects for a ride. On the other hand, girls didn't wait long for a ride regardless of where they were standing. I could have put a dress on Mike and he would have been gone in 10 minutes — well, maybe 15!

As we talked we tried to endear ourselves to the girls. I commented they would certainly catch a ride before us. I requested if they would ask the guy who stopped for them if we too could hop in. "Sure" was the response. It wasn't a long wait before the inevitable ride stopped, the girls jumped in, and the car sped off. I don't think they had time to make a request on our behalf if they had wanted to. On the other hand, they may not have cared. For all the talk of "love", in the 60's and 70's, (other than the physical) we had seen little tangible evidence of it on the road. Treachery was more the rule. I acknowledge I had committed some similar acts in Wyoming but I reasoned they were out of desperation and isolated. I suppose everyone had an excuse.

The day had been a long one and as the evening wore on, Mike and I surrendered to the likelihood we would be spending the night out on the road — in "no man's land". We made one last trip to the gas station for water, returned to our spot on the roadside, and began to seek out a campsite not far away. Our conversations were much more light-hearted and hopeful during this period. We lay in our sleeping bags and talked until Mike no longer responded, signaling his departure.

The desert summer sun is merciless and by 9:00 a.m. we were hurting. We were employing all the tricks we knew to secure a ride. Trying to appear non-threatening, polite, and straight. We also distanced ourselves from the others without venturing too far into the desert. Nothing was working. Hundreds of cars passed by without the slightest indication they were considering stopping or looking us over. In fact, many would accelerate when passing us! The situation, since first light, was growing progressively dismal.

"Mike, let's take any ride that stops," I declared. "Our map shows no towns out there in the middle of the desert. They would *have* to be going through to the next town. We've seen the desert. There are no stores or homes where someone would stop or end the ride."

"I don't know," Mike cautioned. "Everyone said not to do it." Mike's and my disposition sometimes reminded me of an old cartoon series. Baby-boomers may recall "Lippy the Lion" and "Hardy-Har-Har". Best friends, Lippy, of course, was a lion and Hardy was a neurotically worried hyena. Lippy was usually ready to take a chance while Hardy was very quiet and cautious —always expecting the worst. "Oh, I don't know Lippy, I don't think we should," was Hardy's common refrain.

We talked for a while and decided to go for it. It had been hours and no one had even hinted at stopping. Soon after, an old red pick-up stopped for us. A man in his 30's, I would guess, along with his dog, occupied the cab. He motioned with a thumb over his back movement to climb in the bed. We joyfully complied and welcomed the 60 mph wind in our faces. We hadn't even asked where he was going, something we always did. "I'll bet he's going all the way to Las Vegas, " I leaned over and spoke into Mike's ear. He smiled and nodded.

Approximately 50 miles into the desert, we felt the pickup slow and the driver began to pull off the interstate and onto the shoulder. Mike and I looked at each other in bewilderment. I wondered if he was having mechanical trouble. He continued to pull off the road, stopped and motioned for us to unload!

"What's wrong?" I asked the driver.

"Nothing," he responded. "This is where I turn."

"Turn," I thought, turn where, there were no roads, no houses, no stores! Only the interstate and sand. Mike and I unloaded our gear and climbed out of the truck. In disbelief, we watched as the driver drove off across the terrain toward the horizon, with nothing in sight, leaving a trail of dust. With the exception of one lonely gas station situated ½ mile down an unpaved trail, this looked like Death Valley — sand, cactus and intense heat. We had been dropped off in the middle of the Mohave Desert!

It was 10:30 a.m. and the temperature, we had learned at the gas station, was 115 degrees! We had discussed this contingency at length — at least "at length" for teenagers. No way! Never happen! Impossible! Yet here we were. Not at the edge of a town, not even near a town, but far out in the desert's heartland with no shade!

Mike and I had spent our share of time in the sun, shirtless all summer — Lewis' Lake, the trek to California, and the dreadful day in San Diego, but nothing like this! Our bodies were depleting our fluid reserves in minutes. Thankfully, the gas station would prevent our death and we now soberly acknowledged death was in the realm of possibilities in this harsh environment. Our fellow hitchhikers had flatly warned us. "Don't do it!" "Don't make that mistake!" "You can really get into trouble!" Their words echoed in our ears.

The gas station, though a life-saver, also presented problems. We had no choice but to make regular and frequent visits there for water, yet by the time we returned to our hitchhiking post, a half mile's hike in the incredible sun and heat, our mouths and throats were bone-dry again. We were spending fifty percent of our time on water runs. On our last trip back from the gas station, Mike, instead of joining me on the road, walked, with purpose, straight out into the desert. Well, not really "walked"... more like a defiant prance. He continued into the desert like an actor taking his place on stage, dramatically removing his T-shirt and waving it several times in the air. I remember thinking it dangerous to be expending energy and water for this silly charade but Mike seemed determined to see it through. I also realized, as Mike carefully wrapped and tied his shirt on his head in turban fashion, that he effectively ruled out any reasonable chance of us securing a ride. People were leery enough of hitchhikers. Now we appeared as one fairly normal-looking guy hitchhiking while his hippie friend seemed to be high on some kind of powerful drug — maybe acid — while prancing in the deadly heat!

Mike persevered, gradually captivating me. He beautifully executed his desert dance, twirling, arms above his head as if holding a sphere, then up on his toes with short quick steps, followed by a collapse of his upper body in a bow, arms dangling lifelessly towards the ground — then suddenly erect and graceful again in a resurrected burst of strength!

We were healing. Our pain and suffering was becoming increasingly dilute with each mile eastward.

Looking back I realize while the desert dance, at first blush, was funny and frivolous, there was something more profound there. Whether Mike knew it or not, he was telling our story.

Jacob Sparks

Chapter 14
Las Vegas

Mike's dance toned down to a sort of "Tiptoe Through the Tulips" fairy-like saunter, yet he continued to resist my attempts to summon him back to the road — or reality. As a powerful thirst pressed hard on me, I glanced back at the gas station. My attention was drawn to a distinctive old black car exiting the pumps. Even at this distance, I could see and hear it had been "rode hard". I called to Mike to stop the theatrics as I had hopes this might be our ride. Mike continued to dance and at this point I seriously began to wonder if he was okay. I was nearly ready to collapse standing still in the stifling heat while Mike was picking up his pace! He had been at it a half hour. Indeed, the car turned our way and as it neared our position, the massive old black Cadillac began to slow down. The car looked 35 feet long, had no muffler or hubcaps, and was replete with scrapes and dents prominent on all visible surfaces. I'm sure the vehicle turned some heads when it was brought home from the dealer. I'm confident it still turned heads. From my perspective it appeared to be a limo and driver.

"Mike!" I shouted. "Mike!" I had to call several times to bring him back to his senses. "Come on man, we've got a ride!" Had Mike not had me along as a caretaker I believe he might have been found in the desert the next day, red as a berry and hard as a carp!

We peered into the car before climbing aboard. As I've mentioned, we had heard many stories of scary encounters and this ride looked like it had all the makings of one. The driver was a Hell's Angel, a big man, wearing his colors. He had silver chains hanging from everywhere. His neck, his wrist, his vest pockets, across his back, and of course on his huge wallet. He sported big, wavy, iron-like hair and a full beard. He looked like a Celtic chieftain from the Viking days — very intimidating. His girlfriend or "old lady" (as the bikers affectionately refer to them) sat close by him, serene and sedate. I wondered about all the chains dangling from this man. What did they represent? Were they sort of a grown-up and wicked version of Boy Scout badges — for a lucrative robbery — or, maybe his first victorious knife-fight? They must have weighed five pounds in total. Heaven forbid he should ever get hung up in his motorcycle. I assume he had one. I think the Cadillac was more his touring car.

It was mid-afternoon and the desert sun made that day back in San Diego seem pleasant. The heat was the worst Mike and I had ever experienced. The Cadillac had no air conditioning (operable) and the driver held onto the black steering wheel with rags. There was an ashtray in the car that was holding a tube of chapstick. The chapstick had melted and was pooled in liquid form in the ashtray bottom. Indeed it was hot in the car but certainly better than standing in the desert. We had shade and all the car's windows were down, allowing the wind to provide a welcomed buffeting.

The driver offered us an ice-cold can of beer he had just purchased at the desert gas station. We readily accepted without a thought as to the alcohol content aspect. Nor did it necessarily matter that it was ice cold. It was drinkable fluid and that was our only criterion. When I touched the can to my mouth for a drink, I instantly went on auto-pilot and drained it in seconds. In stark contrast, I looked over to see Mike sipping his beer slowly, like an elegant woman at a tea party! Composed and collected, I couldn't believe this was the same guy who was demonstrating classic psychosis just minutes earlier in the desert! The driver stopped a couple of times at fruit stands and we all indulged ourselves. He and his girlfriend were surprisingly congenial and pleasant despite their rogue appearance. Of course Mike's and my standards were significantly lower than when we left Iowa. Back home we would have been seriously embarrassed to be riding in this huge junker with this behemoth at the wheel. But now, after all we had seen, we were quite pleased with the arrangement.

The psychological boost we experienced of escaping LA (and soon California) was invigorating. All was well in our world, a strange old feeling! Positive things were happening. Money, food and rides. Most importantly, we were headed home. Little did we know the fire of adversity was not fully extinguished. Within hours we would discover Nevada's policy on hitchhikers made the Nebraska and California Highway Patrol look like the "Welcome Wagon"!

Our ride in the Cadillac would take us all the way to Las Vegas, actually clear through town to the northern edge of the city where the couple turned east on a secondary road. The ride had been devoid of conversation, mostly due to the loud wind noise coming from the windows and also the steady roar of the Cadillac's mufflerless exhaust. We said heartfelt goodbyes to the couple, climbed out of the car and again found ourselves, where else, back in the desert! One would have thought that somewhere along our long, hot journey we would have acquired a canteen. Never occurred to us once!

We had barely taken notice of the attractions and sights as we passed through "Sin City". Famous places and big cities had lost their appeal altogether. It was the country and backwoods atmosphere of Iowa our hearts now longed for. Again, we found the roadside lined with numerous hippies headed back east and again we positioned ourselves at the far (east) end of the group, leaving a significant space between us and the last hitchhiker. Still, we languished till long after dark. Desert air, we learned, heats and cools quickly due to its' arid nature. In the space of just a couple of hours, we had gone from oppressive heat and thirst (no gas station here), to shivering in the cold. We had the shelter and warmth of our sleeping bags; however, we couldn't stand in our sleeping bags and thumb rides! We decided to hitchhike into the night and escape the desert in cool temperatures. Our hope was to be long gone by morning — but it just wasn't happening.

Mike found an old cardboard box, obviously used by one of our predecessors. It was a large box and Mike immediately recognized its value and latched onto it like an old pro. Might have stabbed a rival for it, I mused humorously. I felt a degree of pride as I sensed my boy was "manning up" — learning the hobo ways. He appeared to be taking on an impressive persona. While most hippie hitchhikers were easy-going pot-head types, the road also had its share of the more traditional hobos. Though typically pitiful men with drinking problems, they did pose a threat. Many of them were hardened by their lifestyle and prone to acts of extreme violence with little or no provocation. Mike and I had been intrigued with their stories and nicknames posted on signs or underneath bridges.

We had gone through some significant changes since leaving Iowa. I wondered if we should spend some time in a halfway house when we returned home, at least initially! Maybe Mike should get a big tattoo across his forearm. A highway moniker like "Texas Red". No, we hadn't been to Texas and Mike's hair was brown. "Freebird"? No, too sissy. Had to be something more intimidating. "Road Dog". Yeah, "Road Dog"! A good tattoo like that might just deter a nasty attack somewhere from an incorrigible bum — over a nice box, for instance!

A box's value lay in the ability to quickly vacate it (if your partner snagged a ride), not possible with the sleeping bag. Mike's box was prefolded from past use and he utilized it with a high degree of proficiency. Granted, it was not rocket science — lay on one half and pull the other half over your body — still he made it appear like familiar routine, with admirable skill. He tucked his duffle bag under his head and did what he did so well. He was asleep in minutes.

I hitchhiked until midnight, desperately wanting to escape the next day's searing desert heat. We had no access to water here and had been warned if we ventured back closer to town to take up a hitchhiking position, we would immediately be taken into police custody. We were told Nevada authorities were notoriously aggressive towards hippies and that the Las Vegas police were especially bad.

As I stood there in the desert silence an unusual sight in the distance caught my eye. A line of police cars, lights flashing, was exiting Las Vegas and heading toward the country. It was puzzling. Why would these police be leaving the city? And why so many? The convoy was stretched out for over a mile. I wondered if there had been an escape from a nearby prison. Whatever the emergency, it soon became clear to me that we were likely situated along the route to their destination. As they made the corner and turned our way, the squad fanned out into the desert in a well-rehearsed plan. We *were* their destination! They converged on our location with their search lights trained on us. Though 3 or 4 miles outside of town, we would discover we were still inside the city limits. There were 30 to 40 of us hitchhikers standing there, frozen with fear!

"Mike!" I shouted. "Mike, wake up!" He didn't flinch. "Mike, wake up! Come on, man!"

"Wha-a-a-t?" Mike said in an irritated drawl, as though his mom was waking him up for school.

"Mike, get up man, there's police all over the place! They're here for us!"

Mike opened his eyes, red and glossy, and saw what looked like the entire Nevada National Guard surrounding us! He had gone from deep NREM sleep to some kind of hellish reality in seconds! He recoiled back inside the box and pulled the top over himself as if closing the door to his apartment!

"Don't tell 'em I'm here," was his directive to me.

"What?" I asked incredulously.

"Don't tell 'em I'm here," he repeated.

"Come on Mike, anyone can see you! Besides, we can't get separated. Get up!" I insisted. My previous notion that Mike had attained manly valor was soundly dispelled.

Jacob Sparks

Mike reluctantly arose and surrendered like the rest of us. The police were rough and frightening by design. There were about 20 cars and 30 - 40 officers, all using tactics more suited for suspected murderers. Our hands were cuffed tightly and we were pushed into squad cars. Everyone was terrified, especially the younger members of the group. Mike was displaying his typical high degree of anxiety. Confused, we were trying to read the officer, desperate to get some sense of why we were being taken into custody like wanted felons and just what might lie ahead. Mike was hyper-alert, his body paralyzed, while his eyes darted from me to the driver to the driver's partner, in circuit, without moving his head. A young fellow hitchhiker sitting between me and Mike was on his maiden voyage. He looked as scared as Mike and whispered to me he had 100 hits (doses) of windowpane acid sewn into the lining of his sleeping bag. He frantically asked me what he should do. I told him there wasn't much he could do — either they would find it or they wouldn't. I had my own worries. My juvenile status could cause problems. If the Las Vegas police held me for parental pick up, I would likely be stuck in Nevada until my eighteenth birthday, more than a month away. Both Mike's and my folks had modest incomes and worked. Undertaking a jaunt clear across the country was not feasible. Additionally, Mike might be forced to hitchhike home alone, daunting enough with a partner.

If the Las Vegas police's objective had been to thoroughly traumatize us, the mission had been a success — and we weren't even at the jail yet! The kid with the dope was really in danger. During this era many young people dabbled in drugs like candy without any real appreciation of the serious legal consequences. Drugs were so prevalent on the streets and most of the people who used them were otherwise criminally clean. It was not uncommon to know of some mild-mannered young man receiving a 10-year sentence in prison over a significant drug possession charge such as the one our fellow prisoner could face if the acid was discovered! I feared the dope in the sleeping bag was not a new trick. The police might well be familiar with the practice — or have a drug dog!

The police station was hopping. We were moved from the squad car to a cell, then to the booking room where we were fingerprinted and questioned. They ran a check on us and placed us back in cells. This was the contingency I had quietly feared the entire journey. I knew Mike would likely be released soon, but I prepared myself to spend weeks in a big city jail, far from home!

The dreadful thing about jail, we would learn, was not the confinement itself so much as *who* you were confined with. There seemed to be no discrimination as to who the police grouped together in these holding cells. We hitchhikers (some quite young and naïve) were in a common cell with a motley crew that included men that looked capable of just about anything your imagination could contrive! There would be no sleep that night. Not even for Mike!

The next morning, to our surprise (and great relief), the jailer called Mike and me out together and told us we were free to go. I think the fact that I was so near to 18 years old must have dissuaded them from holding me. We were overjoyed. Our freedom however was somewhat tempered by the fact there would be no ride back to our hitchhiking spot — some 4 - 5 miles away. And we didn't dare thumb rides in the city. I believe that was part of the police's strategy. To hold us through the night and release us mid-morning which would place us at our pre-arrest location (desert) around high noon — with no water! Bummer! But we were free. I wondered about the kid with the acid. I didn't search person to person however when I quickly surveyed the reassembled line of hitchhikers, I couldn't spot him. If he was 16 or younger he likely would not have been released. Or had the drugs been discovered? I worried for him. He looked so young and innocent. I believe my compassion for him signaled my own innocence and decency was being revived at the prospect of being back home soon. It felt good to be leaving "the jungle".

Chapter 15
Going Home

Since beginning our trip, Mike and I had noticed an occasional hitch-hiker would display a makeshift sign indicating his destination. We realized this might be a good idea for us. Someone returning to Iowa or the Midwest from a vacation might have mercy on a couple of Iowans. We tore off a part of Mike's box, still sitting where we had left it, and went straight to a guy holding a sign that read NY. Our hunch was right. He had a marker in his bag that he let us borrow. Along our journey, when people had asked where we were from and we responded "Iowa", the reaction had been a furrowed brow, a laugh, or "Oh, where they grow the corn!" Our state's motto was The Tall Corn State, and we shamelessly exploited that hee-haw status for personal gain. We added some humor and flare and printed our sign.

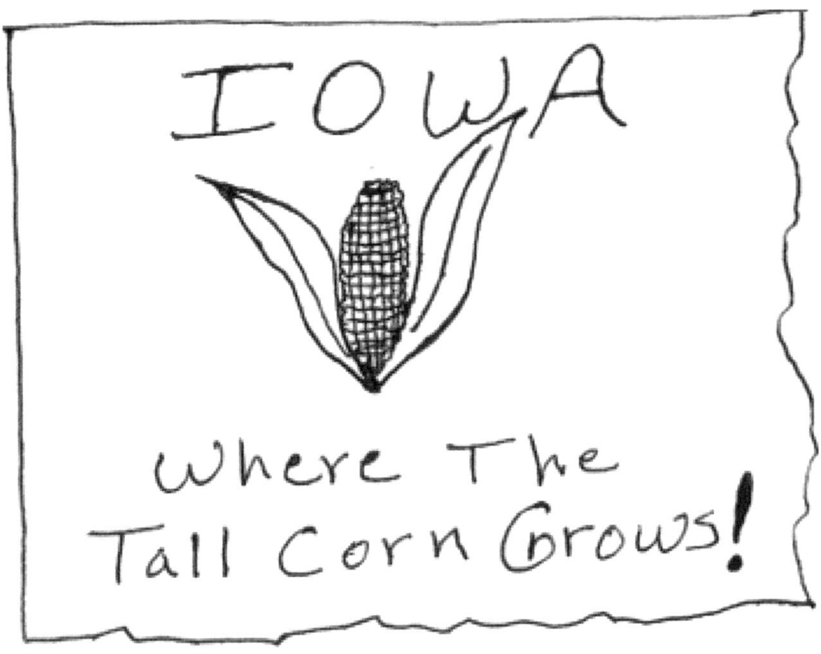

We also saw an advantage in diminishing people's fears. How dangerous could you be coming from "The Tall Corn State"? Our fellow hitchhikers gave their approval of our sign and passersby concurred with honks, smiles, and waves. We knew we had found a priceless tool in securing a ride and a distinct advantage over the other hitchhikers. And none too soon! We were approaching midafternoon and as we had learned, you can't survive long in the summer desert with no shade or water. When we experienced these extended periods of stress, no sleep, walking for incredible periods such as the Seal Beach/San Diego fiasco and now after standing in a jail cell all night, no one needed to remind me of the big plantar's wart on the bottom of my foot. The pain became excruciating! A 35-year-old would have been in traction, or at least a "blue boot" and crutches! Yet a teenager walks halfway to California and back virtually unscathed. I don't believe Mike was even aware of my problem.

We separated ourselves from the crowd some distance and prominently displayed our sign. Within an hour, a single man in a nice (air-conditioned) car* slowed, took a look at us and the sign, and stopped.

As we pulled out onto the road I turned and looked out the back window at the hitchhikers left behind, baking in the sun. A microcosm of what was going on all over the U.S. Like the pitiful young innocents we had left in the field in Nebraska, they were all convinced they were enjoying some supreme liberation from society — a blissful, wayfaring freedom — when, in fact, they were simply victims of media and music propaganda. The counter-culture trend of not working, hitchhiking across the country, doing drugs and following rock bands had a heavy price tag. I pictured Mike and myself still standing with the others on the road. In contrast, the conformist, "plastic" world didn't seem bad at all! A 9-5 job was looking better all the time! We vowed any future trip would be in our own vehicle with adequate funds.

**A surprisingly smaller percentage of vehicles on the road had air-conditioning in 1971 as compared to nearly all cars today.*

Going Home

We introduced ourselves to our new host. We didn't disclose the dark history of our trip. There seemed to be no point in doing so. We were going home and our disposition was very upbeat. We told him our names and that we were from Iowa. We related we had been to California to visit and were looking forward to going home. He said his name was John and he was heading east. Very generic. We could have nearly guessed both those things before getting in the car.

John asked a series of questions which seemed to clearly surpass what would have been appropriate. How old we were. Did we have driver's licenses? Did we still live at home with our parents? At a certain point in the exchange John seemed satisfied. Mike and I noticed the unusual nature of his questions and thought he may have been being vigilant as to whom he shared his car with. Still, the questions seemed excessive and overly-specific.
John offered no information about himself. Where he lived, exactly where he was going, or where he had been. Nor did he tell us what he did for a living or if he had a family. At least Mike had offered no denial when I told John we both had drivers' licenses. We had taken on a more no-nonsense demeanor since Mike had pulled that trick in Cheyenne. At this juncture I believe Mike would have peddled us home on a rickshaw!

When we pressed John on where he was going, he would not provide a definitive answer, other than "back east." We told him, though our sign said Iowa, we preferred to take I-70 east so as to be able to leave me at my parents' home in Missouri. John did not disclose his projected route to us, which held us in suspense. We were ecstatic, however, that the ride looked like it would take us all the way to the Midwest! We had desperately hoped for something like this. Our rides, with the exception of Beth and Linda, had been dismal indeed, mostly for short distances and fraught with danger and despair. Getting dropped off in the middle of cities, desert locations, or places with overly aggressive police had been commonplace.

It wasn't long before John asked if one of us would like to drive. I volunteered and John said he would occupy the backseat as he wanted to check his map and route plans. Mike joined me in the front seat and off we went. John told me to stay on I-15 north for the time being. Mike and I agreed we would modify our projected route to the Midwest to coincide with John's. In retrospect I believe it was John who adapted his course to match ours.

Mike and I were both surprised that within an hour of climbing in, we were driving a complete stranger's car while our host was in the backseat. Beth and Linda had done something similar but they were young and had a relatively obvious and valid reason for doing so.

John was older than Mike and me. Likely in his thirties. He was clean–cut and casually well dressed. He seemed intelligent and wore his hair in a shorter, conservative fashion. He sat in the backseat and carefully scrutinized his U.S. road map. I remember thinking that his route planning on the road seemed odd. Roughly an hour later, John asked me to stop at the next rest area. After using the restroom and getting a drink, John summoned us to take a seat at a picnic table. He wanted to detail to us the route we would take east. It was great news — with a snag. Yes, we were going to track along I-70 but not drive I-70 itself. John had mapped out a path on state and county roads that paralleled I-70. I knew immediately what that meant. Beth and Linda included some of that in our trip west and it appreciably added length and time, not to mention poorer road conditions.

John revealed to us he had recently been working long hours and would appreciate it if we did a fair amount of the driving while he caught up on sleep. We quickly agreed to accommodate even though we had had no sleep the night before in the Vegas jail. I wanted so badly to be home and never leave the state again, I was willing to drive straight through! We were two days from Columbia, Missouri, if we drove continuously. To drive along these lesser roads would increase the trip length by an additional day or two. But it was something John had insisted on. He said the route would take us past some beautiful sights that would be missed altogether if we took the interstate.

We headed north into Utah, John sleeping in the backseat and Mike and I in the front. We were excited and again running on adrenalin. We had almost $10 left and decided we could forego the peanut butter sandwich diet and simply project the length of our trip and divide the time by hamburger and fries meals. We hadn't learned a thing!

Mike and I reflected on our time at Holy Cross Mission. We couldn't forget Bob, the white knight in the nightmare. I don't know about Mike but I had prayed before in my life — at night while lying in bed. I had an innate sense of God, as I think everyone does, yet Bob's connection to Jesus seemed different. Mike and I would talk about Bob during the trip back home. We both had a curious envy as to what he had found in the Book of John.

As we snaked through Utah and Colorado, Mike and I saw sights that were astounding — while John slept. He awoke only when we roused him to pay for gas at pit stops. He would immediately ask if we were staying strictly on the roads he had designated. Some of these roads were absolutely terrifying. Around mountains on hairpin curves with poorly maintained shoulders or virtually none at all! Looking over, where the shoulder should have been, it was not unusual to see a sheer drop of hundreds of feet! And by this time I hadn't slept for 2 days! Mike would drive occasionally but it was usually for just a couple hours. I didn't mind as I couldn't sleep well in the car and additionally we had an increasing reason for concern. We would soon be across Colorado and it became clear John's story was phony.

For instance "John" had explained the reason for taking side roads was so he could take in the sights. The only sight John was seeing was the upholstery on the backseat! Moreover, John had us slated to continue to stay on the side roads through Kansas. All due respect to my birth state, the Kansas landscape, like Nebraska, is dull regardless of which road one travels! We agreed while waiting on a burger at a gas station-restaurant in central Kansas — John was on the run. There could be no other explanation. Why else would someone let strangers drive his car across the U.S.? Why avoid the major highways? Why lie to us about the sights? Clearly John was having us drive so he could stay out of sight in the backseat. It seemed highly unlikely that he was sleeping the whole time, by then for over 2 days! Were we driving a stolen car? Or a car with a bogus license plate? What was in the trunk of the car? A suitcase of cash? Drugs? A body? Did John have a gun under the seat? We knew he was running, likely from something very serious! We also knew we could be in danger. Still, after all we'd been through and considering how badly we wanted to get home, we decided to roll the dice. We were obviously serving a vital function for John. Harming us would ruin that for him. And even if he *was* on the run, what reason would he have to harm us when the time for our departure came in Columbia? We posed no threat. We just hoped John shared our reasoning. We also hoped he was not a traveling serial-killer whose only brand of reasoning was who he could conveniently kill next!

We hadn't exchanged more than a few sentences of dialogue with John during the entire trip, which had spanned approximately 1,500 miles! He didn't fit the profile of your typical crook or gangster. His well-groomed appearance and intelligence distinguished him from common street criminals. He drove a nice family car. In retrospect, I believe he may have killed someone in an act of passion (perhaps an unfaithful wife). Maybe he was a high-class bank robber. Possibly a Ponzi scheme con-man whose deception had just been discovered. Whatever the case, John would forever remain a mystery.

We neared the Highway 63 intersection at Columbia, Mo and I pulled off the road. John crawled out of the backseat, and with little fanfare, said goodbye and drove away.

Hitchhiking was well tolerated by authorities in both Missouri and Iowa. With only 100 miles to my folk's house and another 150 more for Mike to get home, our worries were over. I could almost smell Mom's "light rolls" baking!

Chapter 16
The Gift

We walked into my folks' yard in the beautiful Missouri countryside and were greeted like gladiators returning from the arena! What they didn't know was that we had lost — or at least we thought we had.

"How was your trip? Tell me *all* about it," my mother inquired excitedly.

Where would I start? Where would I stop? It was like war. Like a lifetime of adventure, despair, tragedy, and crisis, all packed into a few weeks! Additionally, all aspects of the trip seemed integral and defied dissection. To properly recount the entire journey would have taken days — and it deserved nothing less. Mike and I knew they wouldn't get it. How powerful it was. How hard it was. We never even attempted to detail the excursion to our families or others. That is with one exception —— Bob. I told my mom about this wonderful man at a Christian mission in LA who told us exciting things about Jesus and the "Holy Spirit".

At long last we were out of harm's way. The beds were luxurious. Same old beds but they felt different now. "Meal choices" — upon request! And, of course, the babying my mother was lavishing on us. So safe from desert heat, strangers, and the "men in blue." All the things I previously had taken for granted I now deeply appreciated — like Snoopy!

We listened to our favorite music, the Beatles, while I played along on the drums — the ones I had sold my beat up 1956 Ford Fairlane to get. Actually I had given the matter careful consideration. I reasoned girls would be far more impressed with my drum-playing than an old rust bucket. It was only *after* the sale of the car that I recognized the resultant inability to drive these admirers around or take them out on dates. Bummer! I guess I thought they would find their own transportation to my house (in the country) for private concerts (those frontal lobes still only hitting on a couple of cylinders)!

Jacob Sparks

Summer had ended and with the coolness in the air came a wistful feeling. Mike and I had no place to go — nowhere to be. No structure or schedule existed at all in our lives and no plans whatsoever for the future. Societal disconnect, uncertainties, and apprehensions plagued us. Our peers were scheduled for work or college, but not us. We felt totally alienated — again! Thumbing on the highway of life — destination unknown!

Meanwhile, Mike and I received our draft numbers. Mine was around 350 while Mike's was in the single digits. We misinterpreted the information thinking it was the high numbers who would be called. Of course I was concerned with my status as the Vietnam War was still active. In contrast, Mike reveled in the news with taunts and quips directed at me. That is, until a few days later when we discovered we had it backwards. Low numbers would be called. It was Mike who would be drafted! He decided to enlist in the navy as enlistees had benefits over those who were drafted. I was leaning toward following my dad in the electrical trade. But first I promised myself a hiatus at home to lick my wounds from the trip.

Before Mike and I were to split up and go out into the big scary world we spent a week at my folks' house. Soon Mike felt the need to push on north, the last few hours, to be reunited with his family. He pressed me to go with him. Kind of like walking him home, I guess. I agreed and off we went. Back on the road — but 150 miles was kid-stuff.

The reunion with Mike's family was a replay of mine. Everyone treating us like conquistadors and us feeling like a couple of General Custer's men who had barely survived the carnage. I spent a couple days at Mike's place before returning home.

Plantar's Wart update:

Following my return to Missouri I had a doctor remove the plantar's wart from the bottom of my foot. Worst pain I'd ever experienced in my life — thought I was going to die! It grew back to its full size within 3 weeks. Bummer!

I couldn't forget Bob's stories about Jesus. Back at home I found an old Bible and began to look it over. It was a King James Version, one that was printed in Early Modern English — "thee", "thou", and "shalt". Difficult terms for a 17-year old to connect with. I later found the New King James Version* to be much simpler.

It didn't take long, however, before I could speak "Early Modern English." I began listening less to rock and roll and was drawn rather powerfully to the Bible. I would recline on my bed, leaning against the headboard, and read, and read, and read... Indian summer prevailed and my room was on the 2nd floor of the home. There was a door in my room that allowed access to the 1st floor roof and I would take reading breaks there and enjoy the starry skies. I looked at them more closely now that I was coming to know God. I was consumed, however, by three emotional and co-existing considerations in my life. Having to go out into the world on my own, wondering about (and in wonder of) Bob, whom I could not forget, and also an irresistible energy that compelled me to read the Bible.

I continued to read, each night, sometimes until 4 or 5 o'clock in the morning. The story of Jesus overwhelmed me. This gospel (Book of John) that Bob had pursued so fervently for three years was seemingly being made manifest to me in a shorter space of time. Additionally, I would lose myself in the stories of Paul the Apostle (beginning in the Book of Acts) whose adventures took him far beyond the borders of Israel to share the good news of Jesus with Greeks, Asians, and others. Paul regularly suffered imprisonment, beatings, stoning, shipwreck, and many tests of faith and strength as he boldly persevered, full of the Holy Spirit! I was filled with love for Jesus and a desire to follow Him. I wanted to be just like Paul!

**I also believe the New King James Version to be, by far, the most accurate of the contemporary translation choices today — though the King James Version is preferable (if understood) in terms of originality.*

My life had changed dramatically in just a few short weeks. I had transformed from a wild and reckless teenager into a thoughtful and dedicated student of the Bible. Studying scripture became my compulsion with God granting me remarkable insight and understanding, despite my age. Learning about and connecting with Jesus became my foremost concern in life — happily secluded and perfectly at peace in my makeshift monastery in Missouri!

Some denominations believe when an individual comes to Christ, professes their faith, and asks for forgiveness for sins, that person instantly receives the gift of the Holy Spirit. This is, I believe, a widespread misconception in the Christian community. One that effectively precludes a number of Christians from praying for the Holy Spirit, having been taught or led to believe they have already attained it. Similarly, some churches teach that all members of the congregation have been blessed with the Holy Spirit simply by virtue of being in attendance, and again I don't believe that to be true. God tells us in the Bible, "And ye shall seek me and find me when ye shall search for me with all your heart." The key (at least for Bob and me) was in reading the New Testament, relentlessly and daily. There is nothing as powerful as the word of God — the unspeakable peace of you, Jesus, a lamp, and the Bible. Bob had planted a seed in me that was watered through reading the Bible in my Missouri bedroom — and soon I received the gift Bob had sought and secured. It was unmistakable and the most powerful force I had ever experienced. Far more so than the lure of the twins. As evidence of that, I was ready to undertake the dreadful proposition of returning, hitchhiking alone, to LA and reuniting with Bob.

Bob's memory was ever-present in my mind. He was full of the love of Jesus and the Lord was his sole concern. How he might help save people. He had no formal education. He certainly did not pastor in a beautiful church. He had no staff or elders. I doubt he received any salary at all. His clothes were old and worn. He had no automobile. His "flock" was homeless men with addictions, the vast majority of whom attended solely for food. Yet Bob was undaunted, preaching fervently and with the utmost devotion, his eyes aglow with the Spirit of God. He was a well-spoken, intelligent man whom I'm confident could have secured a good paying job, wife, family and home. Instead, he chose to forego those things and live in a small (cell-like) room in a shabby building and eat outdated sandwiches, I assume until he died. As Christians we sometimes struggle to give our ten percent tithing. I don't think Bob *kept* ten percent of anything he received! Looking back I have no doubt he fervently prayed for the souls of Mike and me. When I remember Bob I can't help but think of John the Baptist, who wore an animal skin for clothing, ate locusts and honey, and lived in the wilderness — to save souls —denying himself virtually all the comforts of life.

I don't know exactly how many angels inhabit "Los Angeles" — but I can say, with certainty, in the summer of 1971 there was a man of God there!

Chapter 17
"...stood a Lamb..."

Bob had revealed to me and Mike a Jesus we never knew. The Bible was confirming Bob's testimony and expounding great and wonderful things about this Man whose *name* we all know. But not simply the "Jesus" who was born in Bethlehem, grew up quickly, died on the cross and was resurrected. I believe people generally and even many Christians are not aware of the suffering Jesus endured on a daily basis, long preceding the cross. A Jesus who was afflicted from the earliest age. The One with a price on His head His entire life (remember Herod's edict*?). He was perpetually conspired against, living in fear of being beaten, stoned, jailed, or murdered before He accomplished His mission. Constantly in danger of ambush virtually any time He was in public, as the forces of Satan plotted. Pharisees, scribes and priests, engaging Him in dialogue, sought to entrap Jesus in heresy or words that could be construed to violate Roman law. That would open the door for crucifixion, something the Jews badly wanted but lacked authority to carry out.

It is sad to think about the tangible reality of Jesus' hardships, such as NKJV Matthew Chapter 8, Verse 20 when Jesus (probably exhausted and hungry) said, "...Foxes have holes and birds of the air have nests, but the Son of Man has nowhere to lay His head." Sometimes at night, as I lay in bed, I have to wonder why I am given this comfort while the Son of God slept on the hard ground! Then I'm reminded of the words of Isaiah, KJV Chapter 53 Verses 4&5 "...He has borne our griefs, and ... sorrows ...." also "...He was wounded for our transgressions, ...", speaking of Jesus' life and death on earth. In addition, I'm confident He was malnourished much of His adult life.

* *King Herod, with murderous intent, requested the three wise men inform him of baby Jesus' whereabouts. When Herod realized his request had been disregarded he issued the order that all male Jewish children in the region under the age of two years be killed, casting a death net that would surely eliminate this "newborn King"!*

Numerous examples in the Bible confirm Jesus' preference to preach salvation rather than eat, such as Matthew Chapter 12, Verse 1. This scripture depicts Jesus and his disciples, hungry, as they journeyed through a cornfield. His disciples picked and ate some of the corn — but not Jesus — though, no doubt, He was as hungry as His companions. On another occasion His disciples urged Him to eat, which I believe was commonly required — KJV John, Chapter 4, Verse 31: "In the meanwhile his disciples prayed Him, saying, Master, eat." Jesus explained to them saving souls was more important than food. When I finish a big delicious meal (one of many) I should always remember how seldom it was that Jesus was indulged in the same. How many times did He forego a meal for the sake of making it to the next town, before dark, to save more souls?

Jesus' life must have been similar to what homeless people endure, only worse. No home. No bed. No certain source of food, medicine, or bathing facilities. I'm confident Jesus was indistinguishable from the homeless people we see on our streets today. What Mike and I had barely survived for a few weeks was Jesus' routine. I can't imagine, additionally, being publically hated, hunted, and persecuted 24-7- 365!

Scripture tells us Jesus knew, explicitly, vividly, and down to the minute detail, the specific acts of the torture which would lead to His death. He knew how many lashes would be laid upon His back (was it really necessary to beat Him before nailing Him to the cross?). He knew His beard would be yanked out! He knew how many hours this torture would continue before He was led away, bleeding and weakened from the abuse, after a night of sleepless terror, to Golgotha — the site He had surely visited so many times in visions. Moreover, He knew exactly what the spikes looked like which would penetrate His flesh. As a carpenter's son I have little doubt Jesus pondered His looming appointment with the cross each time He drove a nail. Jesus knew the final act of His sacrifice was to be suspended from that cross, allowing His torn flesh and the bones of His hands and feet to carry the weight of his body!

I am not a doctor, albeit one can draw some obvious conclusions based on reason and the law of gravity concerning Jesus' ordeal on the cross. Along with the biblical accounts and Jesus' personal testimony of the details, inferential evidence gives a rather compete picture — despite the "cold-case" status.

Jesus, almost certainly, lost consciousness multiple times, suffering shock from the pain and loss of blood, compounded by His fixed vertical position, before ultimately succumbing to death. It is hard to fathom the pain radiating from Jesus' hands and feet, not to mention His shoulders almost certainly being dislocated from carrying His body weight. I visualize Jesus, turning His head from side to side to view His strangely protruding shoulder bones. He references that, I believe, in Psalms, Chapter 22.

The physicians Merck Manual, 19th Edition, Pg. 3214 describes shoulder dislocation: "Symptoms and signs include pain, swelling, deformity and inability to move. The acromion, (the lateral extension of the …scapula, forming the highest point of the shoulder… Mosby's Medical dictionary, Revised 3rd Edition) is prominent; the humeral head is displaced anteriorly and inferiorly …." Or, in other words, the top of the scapula (shoulder blade) is grotesquely projected above the normal shoulder architecture. I believe there is little reasonable doubt Jesus suffered shoulder dislocation on the cross and His comment that His bones were "out of joint" was likely alluding to that specifically.

Given His dire and grave set of circumstances, I believe, Jesus' most pressing distress would have been the pain in His hands and feet. In addition to the weight of His body hanging on the nails, it would have been necessary for Jesus to lift Himself slightly, pushing off His hands and feet, to get a full breath. Otherwise His diaphragm and lungs would have to lift the weight of His body to breathe. Some physicians conclude Jesus ultimately died of suffocation (I speculate when He was unable to continue executing that maneuver). Sadly, the procedure to breathe would further injure His hands and feet, already traumatically inflamed and swollen. Add to that the effect of gravity progressively pulling His shoulders out of joint. His grim choice was to either breathe by levering off the nails in His hands and feet, thereby completely dislocating His shoulders — or not breathe! We can assume He chose to breathe, losing the battle with gravity over His shoulders, eventually leaving His arms paralyzed. Ironically, I believe it was the tormented process of breathing that induced Jesus' suffocation! Though, no doubt, my medical observations surpass my qualifications, I believe we can agree Jesus suffered an incredibly painful and torturous death!

A comprehensive biblical review of the crucifixion lends a more vivid image of the powerful and dramatic sacrifice Jesus Himself foretold of — a thousand years prior to His earthly death — NKJV Psalms Chapter 22, verse excerpts as follows, give snapshots of Jesus' misery on the cross, in His own words:

My God, My God, why have You forsaken Me?

Why are You so far from helping Me,

And from the words of My groaning?

>>>

But I am a worm, and no man; A reproach of men, and despised by the people. All those who see Me ridicule Me; They shoot out the lip, they shake the head, saying, "He trusted in the Lord, let Him [God] rescue Him; [from the cross] Let Him [God] deliver Him, since He delights in Him!"

>>>

Be not far from Me,

For trouble is near;

For there is none to help.

>>>

I am poured out like water,

And all My bones are out of joint; [shoulders – possibly wrists and elbows?]

My heart is like wax;

It has melted within Me. [circulatory distress from shock?]

My strength is dried up like a potsherd,

And My tongue clings to My jaws;

>>>

They pierced My hands and My feet;

I can count all My bones.
They look and stare at Me.

>>>

I don't pretend to have ever known the depth of physical suffering Jesus endured but I have had a hint or two…

It all began one day with a trivial discomfort in my abdomen. I continued the project I was working on and as the day progressed, the *benign* stomach pain established itself as a serious contender for my attention. I moved with difficulty and ultimately realized the E.R. down the street would supplant my plans for a nice dinner in the house after a hard day's work.

Following an exam and C.T., the E.R. doctor diagnosed appendicitis. Good — and bad. We had definitively identified the source of the pain … however, a surgery was indicated. Things followed a very dire course from that point on … I would literally be pleading for the surgery as hours dragged on. The first problem was the surgeon–on-call made a decision to defer my surgery until the following day as the C.T. scan revealed the appendicitis to be at a non-urgent level (I wasn't aware appendicitis came in a "non-urgent" form). The kind E.R. physician, however, comforted me with a promise to admit me to the hospital and liberally administer morphine to control the pain.

What we discovered in the aftermath of this disaster, was an idiosyncratic and paradoxical reaction to the pain medication — known as "Sphincter of Oddi spasm"! This abdominal spasm can cause unbearable pain and was induced (and maintained) with each successive dose of morphine.

We were all perplexed as my loud cries of agony could be heard down the hall. The nurses, compassionate and near tears, were hyper-diligent to be punctual for each dose of the morphine, having no idea the drug was the source of the incredible suffering. Following each "push" of Morphine into my IV, the pain would intensify, coming in colicky waves that actually made me wish for unconsciousness or death. I didn't care which.

The next morning the surgeon arrived and to my great distress, informed me my surgery would follow his pre-scheduled patients' surgeries, later in the afternoon! The extreme pain (and Morphine) would continue!

Jesus' pain had to be every bit as severe as mine, and likely much worse. I was in awe as I lay there thinking of Him and how He could have ended it at any moment. His place with God would have been secure. He did this for *us*. I love Jesus and God with all my heart, however, I could never imagine having the strength to persevere and continue the torture that Jesus endured had I seen an open door*. I'll never forget the horrifically vivid taste of what Jesus endured "… unto death …"

Scripture indicates Jesus always had explicit foreknowledge of the painful torture — Psalms-Chapter 22 – Isaiah Chapter 50

**incredibly though, God can give us the strength to suffer and die (prophets, disciples, apostles and other martyrs) when the time comes.*

Verse 6. How could He ever have peace, knowing, so well exactly what agony laid ahead? For years in human form on earth and timelessly, as evidenced in His dialogue 1000 years prior to His crucifixion (Psalms Chapter 22). How many nights when Jesus traversed the Holy Land did these mental videos play, robbing Him of sleep? Frequently He would indicate His dread and preoccupation concerning His commissioned destiny with comments to His companions that were entirely unrelated to the conversation — such as KJV Luke Chapter 9, Verse 44. Out of the blue, Jesus states, "… the Son of man shall be delivered into the hands of men." Similarly, KJV Matthew Chapter 17, Verses 22 and 23 "…The Son of Man shall be betrayed into the hands of men: And they shall kill Him and the third day He shall be raised again…"

As the time for Jesus' arrest grew close (roughly within an hour — KJV Mark Chapter 14, Verse 37) apprehension seized Him, much like it does us when a major surgery is minutes away. He was scared to death! KJV Matthew Chapter 26, Verse 38 "My soul is exceeding sorrowful, even unto death: …"

Jesus knew Judas (the paid informant) was en route with church leaders and a pre-destined goal of His murder. Frantically, He asked Peter and Zebedee's two sons to watch for the mob as He resorted to a secluded spot in the Garden of Gethsemane to plead with God to take away this dreadful fate. He would then return to check on His friends and seeing the troupe had not yet arrived — return to His place of prayer to again appeal to His Father for deliverance.

Jesus did this three times! KJV Luke Chapter 22, Verses 42 and 44: "… Father if thou be willing, remove this cup from me: nonetheless not my will, but thine, be done." "And being in an agony He prayed more earnestly: and His sweat was as it were great drops of blood falling down to the ground." I don't accentuate the angst and desperation Jesus demonstrated to suggest He was spiritually weak-willed or lacking resolve. I do it to illustrate our Lord was in human

Jacob Sparks

form and His anxiety, terror, and distress was exactly what it would have been in you or me! Indeed, He *was* the Lion of the Tribe of Judah. He was also a tender, loving Lamb. Though gruesome fears consumed Him, He voluntarily surrendered His life! Therein lies a powerful essence of the cross.

When we read closely of Jesus's last hours we see the extent of His suffering went far beyond humiliation, a quick whipping, and death on the cross. Such as when a few of the soldiers escorted Jesus into the "common hall" to afflict him — then called to the entire band of soldiers to join in the abuse and torture! I have a sense this is the scene that came to Jesus' mind when he had earlier predicted all His followers would forsake Him and "leave Me alone: …" Jesus goes on to say He is really not alone because God is with Him — but sadly, in this ordeal, only in spirit. Jesus' killers' purpose was not only to murder Him but to do so with the highest level of misery and suffering. Additionally, consider God's sacrifice here… handing His Son over to thugs to be tortured to death! Moreover, consider God's reason … to save His adoptive children (you and me), most of whom (unlike Jesus) have been consistently and persistently disobedient from day 1!

I used to be a little vague as to exactly what the biblical term "grace" meant. Jesus' story represents a classic and premier definition — an incredible gift from God we really don't deserve.

Jesus' suffering on the cross was hideous and appalling, yet, again, we should remember His entire life was filled with adversity. The bible articulates a beautifully sad forecast and summary of Jesus's life and the abiding misery He would know — beautiful, of course, for what He would accomplish. Let's hear the story of Jesus in God's words through Isaiah, the Prophet. NKJV Chapter 53 Verses 2-5 & 7-10: "For He [Jesus] shall grow up before Him [God] as a tender plant, and as a root out of dry ground. He has no form or comeliness; and when we see Him there is no beauty that we should desire Him.

He is despised and rejected by men, a Man of sorrows and acquainted with grief. And we hid, as it were, our faces from Him. He was despised and we did not esteem Him. Surely He has borne our griefs and our sorrows yet we esteemed Him stricken, [cursed] smitten by God and afflicted. But He was wounded for our transgressions, He was bruised for our iniquities; the chastisement for our peace was upon Him, and by His stripes [beatings and torture] we are healed. He was oppressed and He was afflicted, yet He opened not His mouth; He was led as a lamb to the slaughter, and as a sheep before its shearers is silent, so He opened not His mouth. He was taken from prison and from judgement, and who shall declare [defend] His generation? For He was cut off from the land of the living; for the transgression of My [God's] people He [Jesus] was stricken and they made His grave with the wicked [convicts]…He had done no violence, nor was any deceit in His mouth…"

Again, all this tremendous sacrifice — so WE might be saved from hell! I believe it is good to consider this selflessness and suffering when we read the popular scripture NKJV John 3:16. "For God so loved the world that He gave His only begotten Son, that whoever believes in Him should not perish but have everlasting life." Fully understanding Jesus' sacrifices in life and death should remove any mundane or boring aspect of John 3:16 one might entertain from redundant hearing of the scripture. I know my understanding of this powerful verse is now more complete— as is the sadness and wonder in the spiritual vision given John the Revelator, concerning heaven and end-day events- KJV Revelations, Chapter 5, Verse 6: "And I beheld, and lo, in the midst of the throne and of the four beasts, and in the midst of the elders, *stood a Lamb* as it had been slain, …"

Though I have written at great length of Jesus' love and sacrifices, I can summarize this entire chapter in 8 words from KJV Isaiah Chapter 53 Verse 12: "…He hath poured out His soul unto death…"

One night as I lay in bed in a motel in the Deep South on a relocation scouting trip, Jesus' love and devotion occupied my thoughts. I mentally penned a poem of gratitude.

Jesus

In every day that I have left
If I should pray from sun to sun,
I would lack a lifetime still,
To thank you Lord for all you've done.

Chapter 18
The Dream – Unveiled

I continued to read the Bible daily which I believe is the key to adherence to a Christian life and salvation. I later discovered neglect of this daily feeding can be spiritually disastrous. I knew decision time was approaching. I desperately wanted to simply continue indefinitely at my folks house, secluded, far out in the Missouri woods and safe from the world. I badly wanted to preserve this precious gift I had received and knew the world would strive to take it away. I understood I was a new Christian and lacked a firm underpinning to insure my walk with God would be sustained. At the same time, I recognized our duty and commission as followers of Jesus was to spread this "good news" to others. I considered going back to LA and devoting my life to preaching to the homeless with Bob. Or, alternatively, going out into the world and learning the high-line electrical trade. I struggled with the differing choices. I knew linemen spent much of their lives on the road. Drinking, sexual promiscuity and ungodly habits and language dominated the lifestyle of many of these men. To be sure, it wasn't as though I had been a stranger to that persuasion. I felt a vulnerability that stood to threaten my newfound treasure.

Ultimately, I chose line work and, as I had feared, was drawn away from God. I would struggle numerous periods in my life, falling away and desperately finding my way back to God. Sadly, (at least according to some statistics) the majority of people who come to God don't stay. When a person surrenders their life to Jesus, the host of heaven rejoice and all forces of hell are called to action. Every tool at Satan's disposal is utilized to derail and rescind the saved status of the new Christian. Some persevere, admirably, with great strength, like Bob. Some relapse into a life of sin and never reconnect. Others, like me, fall away and through grace and forgiveness find their way back. There should be no residual shame in this — at all. God's greatest glory is His forgiveness and it is limitless to those who truly repent. Many examples of the forgiveness afforded backsliders exist, not the least of which is the beloved King David (who admittedly had more sins than the number of hairs on his head!) — or the prodigal son — or for that matter, the Old Testament Jewish nation who at times was famous for its propensity to sin and backslide yet remained most precious to our Lord. God, in His unfathomable grace, loves and forgives infinitely. He is not concerned with how long a person's rap sheet is. His only concern is that a sinner comes back to Him with true repentance. Jesus tells us in NKJV Luke Chapter 17 Verse 4 "And if he [a brother] sins against you seven times in a day, and seven times in a day returns to you saying, I repent, you shall forgive him." We should never let past sins or a backsliding past overwhelm us and prevent a return to God.

Eventually, I would become settled and the seed which Bob planted would become established. I never forgot Bob and the words he gave me. I recall them as vividly today as when he first spoke them, 45 years ago! I hope to see him again in heaven, (his place there is far more certain than mine!)

As I reflect back at the arduous and almost unbearable excursion to California it is clear the trip had a providential framework. God had used the nearly intolerable conditions of the journey that he might have our full and undivided attention. The true treasure and goal was not the pretty twins. Nor was it the ocean. I believe God used the girls to lure us. Had someone told us how difficult the road, heat, and hunger would be — we would have declined the trip. Had someone suggested we endure countless hardships to go to LA, listen to a reformed hobo and live in a dirty mission house, eating outdated and tasteless sandwiches, we would have soundly rejected the offer. Little did we know of the bounty this humble hobo's heart held.

In 1914, Ernest Shackleton, an English explorer, conducted an expedition to Antarctica. The objective was to sail to and then cross the continent on foot. He and his men met with many disasters and ultimately became stranded with no food or provisions in the bitterly cold climate. Months later, Ernest took 2 of his most able men and made a desperate attempt to reach a whaling station on South Georgia Island. On the last leg of the journey, with his two men nearly overcome with exhaustion, Ernest granted their request for a rest/nap atop one of the mountains they were traversing. However, fearing the men might succumb to hypo-thermia, he allowed them to sleep only 10 minutes. When he woke them and they inquired how long they had slept, he replied "30 minutes".

Following the final push on South Georgia Island towards the whaling station, Shackleton recounted a strange sensation he had during the 36-hour trek. "I felt as though we were four and not three. I said nothing to my companions. Harley later said to me, "Boss, I had a curious feeling there was another person with us." The experience Shackleton and his companion testified to strikes a chord with me on two counts. One, it reminds me of the story in the Book of Daniel (Chapter 3) when Nebuchadnezzar, king of Babylon, commanded Daniels' friends, Shadrach, Meshach, and Abednego, to be cast info the fiery furnace for refusing to worship his golden statue. As the king peered into the furnace he proclaimed, "Did not we cast three men bound into the midst of the fire? ...Lo, I see four men loose, walking in the midst of the fire ... and the form of the fourth is like the Son of God."

Two, I believe that same "person" accompanied Mike and me on our entire journey, orchestrating, protecting, and guiding us. Watching over us as we slept. Sending the hippie rescue van in Nebraska just seconds before the trooper returned! Making the Sacramento patrolman do an "about face" on our way to jail there, with no explanation at all! Redirecting us back to LA following the detour to San Diego. Routing us back to Silver who had the crucial advice to go to the Holy Cross Mission — when the time was right. Jesus had to ensure

Jacob Sparks

we were so physically depleted and hungry when we arrived we would not leave the mission without hearing Bob's full teaching. For added assurance to that end He carefully misplaced our rescue money at the post office. And when the true purpose of the trip was accomplished and the seed was planted in our hearts, God spirited us home faster than if we would have had our own vehicle!

For many years I thanked God for this terrible and (ultimately) wonderful experience and was convinced the sole purpose was to communicate salvation to Mike and me — though, granted, it would seem a grandiose production for two solitary souls. I guess you might call that thinking "Christian vanity".

I now perceive the divine goal went far beyond Mike and me. "Seed" is mentioned 279 times in the Bible (KJV). God is clearly a spiritual farmer. As the seed Bob received grew and produced fruit (including me) via the Holy Cross Mission Ministry, the seed I accepted will hopefully find fertile ground on paper, all these years later, and reach countless souls — 'The California Dream (1971).'

EPILOGUE

I received Mike's letter from boot camp near the Great Lakes while still at home pondering my future move. He was miserable in the navy! The letter was concise, containing only four large words that filled the page:

GET
ME
OUTTA
HERE!

(I guess he still considered me the captain.)

I ultimately chose to follow my dad's profession as an electrical lineman. Dad drove me to Washington, Iowa where I was to report for my first "line-job."* He would help me rent a room at the Washington Hotel on the town square, a hotel he had stayed at many times in the past when working in the area. It was an emotional 2 hour trip. I was still 17 and worried about the challenges and responsibilities that would lie ahead — the very next morning! I had seen these line crews before, journeymen who traveled doing the more complex and difficult work that was, for the most part, beyond the scope and talents of "utility linemen." They were strong, skilled, and admirable in many ways, yet could also be rogue and rough with a penchant for practical pranks with little regard for the health or wellbeing of the recipient! Dad, I'm sure, was apprehensive about personally delivering his young son to this sometimes unstable mob.

Dad struck a very strong and fatherly role on the trip, I'm sure to calm my fears. He reviewed a mental laundry list of checkpoints to assure me we had a solid plan and I was covered. Carharts? Check. Gloves? Check. Boots? Check. Hooks? Check. Belt? Check. Then we hit a snag. Dad told me I would be driving trucks, some of them large, and I might also be tapped to operate heavy equipment, such as a backhoe.

"Do you have a good athletic supporter?" The co[illegible] a very personal turn.

"No," I responded, to which Dad looked at me as though I was in the same danger as taking a nap on the ground in front the bulldozer.

"Well, you'd better get one soon," he said with a serious look of concern.

"Okay," I said with total disinterest.

Dad seemed to calm down a little during the next several miles. His composure restored, he returned to a related topic of discussion.

**Within weeks a local native with blonde hair and big blue eyes (and a true heart) would dramatically heal the devastation engineered by Carrie.*

"What kind of underwear do you wear?" he asked, apparently willing to wade into precarious waters again. My underwear status was unknown to him. The question caught me daydreaming about my new job and I answered spontaneously, without thinking.

"I don't wear underwear," I said, impassively.

As the sentence left my mouth I awoke and realized my mistake. Dad's face confirmed the error. If I thought his reaction to my not owning an athletic supporter was bad, I hadn't seen anything yet. His jaw literally dropped open and he stared at me, wide-eyed, as though I had just told him I was addicted to heroin!

"You don't WHAT?" Dad yelled in disbelief at what I had just said.

"I don't wear underwear," I repeated, though more subdued, almost like a question.

"Well, you *will*," he said in total shock, as if it were a life and death matter!

Dad didn't speak again for probably 45 minutes, occasionally glancing at me as though viewing a bad car wreck. I had given him some highly disturbing information to process. He had barely recovered from the no athletic supporter news when I hit him with the more alarming disclosure I did business "au naturel"! I felt a little dejected, which I believe was dad's intention—that I might repent of these barbaric practices and join the crew with both "good athletic supporter" and underwear.

The genesis of my "underwearlessness" dated back to Ronnie's yen to identify with the Hell's Angels. In addition to the desecrated jeans, another dress code requirement for Hell's Angels members was that they wear no underwear. Ronnie encouraged me to get on board. While he quickly and proudly complied with all the mandates, I was reluctant to fully commit. Like many young men, I found, at least to some degree, the counter-culture lifestyle of the bikers to be kind of cool. Fast motorcycles, wild women, no responsibilities, etc. And while Ronnie's observance of Angel Code was very overt, I chose the more limited and private expression of devotion. For the most part, at heart, I was a conservative conformist. However, there was a hidden part of me that was riding shoulder to shoulder with Sonny Barger in unrestrained freedom! There was some truth in my contention to Mike in San Diego. We *had* done some pretty dumb things. This one, unfortunately, had become normal (or abnormal) routine!

I felt kind of bad for dad. I'm sure what he had hoped to achieve on the trip had been disappointing, at the least. I think he had envisioned a touching and protective encounter with his son, departing out into the dangerous world. Additionally a chance, for the first time, to connect both father and son *and* man to man. I believe my underwear deviancy ruined that whole scenario and had dad wondering just what other degrading traits I might have acquired during his periods of absenteeism!

In any event, out into the world I went, BVD-clad, yielding to dad's advice. Life on a line crew was going to be tough enough — I needed all the protection I could get!

In all seriousness, the true comfort and strength I had lay in Jesus, Who would pick me up each time I fell, patiently waiting for me, always with an outstretched hand. Whose spirit would guide me, forgive me, and with "amazing grace", let me outlive my sins*!

Mike and I stayed close over the years, living within a short drive from one another in Iowa and seeing each other on a frequent basis. Although, there were periods in my life when I strayed from my walk with God*, Bob's profound love for Jesus and the words he gave me would, in time, settle me to become dedicated and stable. The Bible tells us to teach our children in the ways of God and they

**At lease the felonious ones!*

**Including a Carrie-like unfaithfulness of my own (sweet Washington girl) though which God has forgiven me for, I have never been able to do (or forget).*

Jacob Sparks

will (ultimately) return to Him. Eventually Mike and I lost touch. It had been years since we had talked. I was in the process of planning to move to a ranch outside a major city in the Gulf of Mexico. The relocation would take me clear across the country. I decided to try to contact Mike. I had lost his number so I phoned the company where he had worked for decades. It was a large metal production plant in Clinton, Iowa. Although the company employed hundreds of people, I was amazed (and amused) that the personnel staff knew immediately whom I was inquiring about. The secretaries giggled and chatted with me about Mike. No longer the "shrinking violet", he had become popular and charming! Unfortunately, they informed me Mike had recently left the company and they weren't sure where he had resettled — other than they heard it was "out of state and far away". Sadly, I resigned myself to never seeing or talking to Mike again.

Prior to relocating I made trips down south to assess the rural areas within a large perimeter of the target city. I decided to focus on a particular area which included a few ranches about 30 miles south-east of town. Near the same time, Mike, who had also lost my phone number, paid for a search of my contact info and called me. I didn't recognize the voice, other than it sounded friendly.

"Do you know who this is?" Mike inquired, then immediately (and perfectly) recited every single French phrase I had taught him 45 years ago on the road! He told me he had moved far away, to which I replied,

"Let me guess the state."

"Bingo!"

I took it a step further and said, "Let me guess the city" naming the large city I had my sights set on. Again, I was right! Even more astonishing was the fact he didn't actually reside in that city but rather the same area I had scouted out some 30 miles to the southeast! The properties I had looked at were approximately 1 mile from Mike's new home! I believe the same guiding force that led us so carefully to the Holy Cross Mission was again at work.

Upon our return from LA, way back when, Mike and I often talked about Bob and the affinity he had created in our hearts for Jesus. We both played guitar and had even written a song for Jesus. Things had now changed. Mike was put off when I steered our conversations to religion. He had grown closer to the world while I had found my way to God. Having known and loved Mike for so long, I felt compelled to reach out to him. I wanted us both to return to LA (figuratively) and reconnect with the innocence and purity of that "first love" (And I don't mean the twins!).

Mike's reaction was firm and uncompromising. He didn't want to discuss religion and when he did, had only disparaging things to say. He informed me his sister had also become involved in a church and regularly bothered him with pleas to consider Jesus.

He commented, "It does seem strange you would both be coming to me with this."

Again, I don't think "strange" or "coincidence" had anything to do with it. Regardless, Mike wouldn't budge. I tried to take him back in time.

"Mike, don't you remember how much we liked Bob and his teaching us about Jesus?"

"What I remember was we wanted some of those sandwiches," was Mike's retort.

"Mike," I pressed, "You believed in Jesus."

"I believe in the Beatles!" Mike replied.

I was hurt, both on a spiritual level (as I understood how much we all need God), and on a personal level because Mike and I had been the closest of friends nearly our entire lives. I was also hurt because Mike was reacting so defensively as though I was an adversary. He reluctantly invited me to his house for a visit but he couldn't connect with me at all. We hadn't had a division like this in nearly 50 years as friends. It was as though he felt I had joined a cult and now embraced some scary and strange doctrine which controlled me and could swallow him up as well!

Because of our years of friendship I was trying hard to convince Mike to return to our thinking, long ago, at Holy Cross Mission. But the harder I pressed him, the more defensive he became. Mike and I stood on opposite sides of the battle line. He was trying to lead me back to our former party days and rock music. He insisted I watch a video of a precocious young man play a difficult number by AC-DC on the guitar while I tried to focus the conversation on Jesus and eternity. Mike was earnestly striving to reignite my interest in worldly things while I was trying to reconnect with the once receptive 18-year-old who had been fascinated with Bob. We both were desperate to save the other from what we each felt was a misguided path with grave consequences. Prior to our visit, Mike had planned a strategy, how to influence me — and I had done the same thing in preparation to "rescue" him! We were both solidly entrenched in profoundly opposed and strongly-held world views, at an age when acquiescence or compromise is rare. The sad aspect was that we both inherently knew that if one *didn't* surrender, the longtime relationship would die.

I believe God speaks to all of our hearts — even short of all the exciting details Bob provided us. We knew, back when, that the chaste life Bob preached was a better course than rock and roll, sex, drugs, alcohol and parties. We had been quick to accept Jesus. It hadn't been that long since we were innocent children. Changing course 180 degrees was easier then. There really wasn't much to give up! That had now changed. Mike had decades of partying and worldly living in his past. He was charismatic, charming, and well-established on the social scene and he knew that for him to now convert would mean a renouncement of his entire past adult life. He also knew to surrender to God would mean forsaking his current lifestyle. There's security in the familiar. There can also be notable fear in the unfamiliar, particularly when it entails a remake of all the foundational underpinning that defines your life.

Mike, steadfast in worldly induration, ended the impasse.

"You probably want to get back to the motel."

Like the old days, (during times of stress) Mike withdrew back into his "box". But this time, I could tell, it *did* have a door — and a lock. "Yeah," I said, "I should be going."

We've lived close to one another for four years now with no further contact. Truly a sad chapter in a story of two comrades who couldn't have been closer. But I also understood — at least to some degree. For Christians, the disassociation by friends and even sometimes family that comes with their dedication to God is not uncommon. The bible clearly foretells of that scenario: KJV 1 Peter Chapter 4, Verse 4, "Wherein they [old friends] think it strange that ye run not with them to the same excess of riot [partying]…"

I drove away from Mike's house like leaving a funeral. A still, ambient sadness filled the car. Though overwhelmed by what felt like the loss of a loved one and friend, I had to remember Mike's spiritual future was far more important. Eternity is a long time. God tells us in the simplest terms, that we might understand …. and be saved: KJV Deuteronomy Chapter 30, Verse 19, "…I have set before you life and death, blessing and cursing: therefore choose life, …"

I pray that the seed Bob planted in Mike is still viable — I pray it will be watered. No doubt the Lord is calling him. He sent three messengers: Bob, his sister, and at last, me.

I close with a personal message to him. "Mike, mon ami, je t'aime — toujours." And a new phrase to remember: "Dieu t'aime aussi!"

"Mike, my friend, I love you — still."

"God loves you too!"